CANON'S FODDER

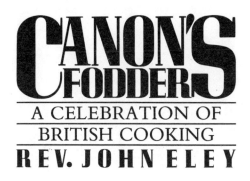

CANON'S FODDER

A CELEBRATION OF
BRITISH COOKING

REV. JOHN ELEY

BBC Books

Design: Eve White
Illustrations: Pip Moon

Published by BBC Books
A division of BBC Enterprises Ltd
35 Marylebone High St, London W1M 1AA

First published 1987
© John Eley 1987

ISBN 0 563 20531 8

Typeset in 11/12 Linotron Bembo by
Rowland Phototypesetting Ltd,
Bury St Edmunds, Suffolk
Printed in Great Britain by
Mackays of Chatham Ltd

· CONTENTS ·

INTRODUCTION

The idea behind this new book of recipes is that it should be a celebration of the simple, tasty and, in the main, economical British tradition of cooking. In my travels up and down the country, giving cookery demonstrations and simply talking to people, I get daily evidence of how much cooking is still enjoyed in this country, how many of the old recipes are still followed, handed on (usually) from mother to daughter, and how eagerly people seek new ideas for making the most of the good, fresh produce our farmers still grow. Thank goodness, not everyone has sold his or her culinary soul to the prepacked, precooked, foil-or-cellophane-wrapped, ready-in-a-minute diet of bland mishmash that thrusts itself at us from every supermarket freezer.

One thing that does seem clear to me is that, given the busy pace of life today, what people are looking for (certainly the ones I talk to anyway) is a simple, no-nonsense approach to food – but they want, too, variety, and the satisfaction of cooking something new and presenting it to their families and friends. Most of us tend to regard food in two different ways – there's the daily problem of refuelling ourselves for work and play, the meal as pit stop; and there's the meal as a social occasion.

Usually it's the woman who has the continual task of thinking up good, basic, balanced meals that will excite her family's taste buds and satisfy their energy needs. Most of us have a stock of standby recipes we fall back on again and again, but let's face it – these can become boring both to prepare and to eat. '*Not* toad-in-the-hole again, Mum!' or macaroni cheese, or liver and onions. I've tried to include, therefore, a number of quick and simple dishes in each section that are easy to prepare at the end of a hard day's work, and won't stretch the family budget too far.

And then there are those times when we sit down to enjoy the pleasures of the table with our friends. And here the problem so often is finding a dish that will seem out of the ordinary and just that little bit extra special but isn't so complicated that it will leave the cook nervous and exhausted so that she's like a frayed piece of string by the time she brings it to the table. Here again I've tried to include something for the occasion. If some of the recipes verge on the extravagant, calling for a luxury item like salmon or pheasant or a joint of beef, cooked with wine or cream or other extra ingredients, then remember we all have times when something really out of this world is called for (and remember, too, that new farming techniques are making some of these items more widely and cheaply available). The most essential ingredient we need then is confidence that the dish is really going to work – and that's why I've looked for recipes that will produce a stunning result without taxing the cook with a stream of complicated instructions.

As the introductions to the various sections in this book make clear, we have in this country a vast store cupboard of good, fresh produce – fish from the sea, meats of all kind, game, vegetables from our back gardens and small holdings, fruit from our fields and orchards. Those of us who live in the countryside are lucky enough to be able to get hold of these things easily when they are in season – even if we don't grow our own we can always pick our own. (And if you've got a glut of anything, then turn to the pickles or drinks section!) But town dwellers have less choice about where to shop. The trouble with supermarkets is that the staff (and I don't believe it's their fault) are uninformed and unenthusiastic about what they sell. I've noticed on my holidays in France that in more and more of their giant superstores the cheese, fish, meat and delicatessen counters are staffed by people who have special knowledge and understanding of the product, and can answer questions about what's on display. I hope that it is a development that may travel over here.

I look forward to the day when we can identify the seasons by what's on sale on the supermarket shelf! One of our troubles is that we have come to expect total availability of all foods at all times, in and out of season – asparagus in December, young lamb all the year round. This makes nonsense of everything – it pushes prices up, and leads to deterioration in standards of flavour. And it destroys the natural pattern that is the basis of our country cooking.

As you look through this cookery book and try out the dishes I hope old memories will be revived, and new tastes enjoyed. It is not meant to be full of the classics, but simply to contain the best of those recipes which people up and down the country have had pleasure in giving me, and which I have delighted in trying out for myself, and sometimes adapting.

My thanks to all of you who have passed on your tips and ideas – and happy cooking.

John Eley

CONVERSION TABLES

All these are approximate conversions, which have either been rounded up or down. Never mix metric and imperial measures in one recipe; stick to one system or the other.

WEIGHTS		VOLUME		MEASUREMENTS	
½ oz.	10 g	1 fl oz.	25 ml	¼ inch	0.5 cm
1	25	2	50	½	1
1½	40	3	75	1	2.5
2	50	5 (¼ pint)	150	2	5
3	75	10 (½)	275	3	7.5
4	110	15 (¾)	400	4	10
5	150	1 pint	570	6	15
6	175	1¼	700	7	18
7	200	1½	900	8	20.5
8	225	1¾	1 litre	9	23
9	250	2	1.1	11	28
10	275	2¼	1.3	12	30.5
12	350	2½	1.4		
13	375	2¾	1.6		
14	400	3	1.75		
15	425	3¼	1.8		
1 lb	450	3½	2		
1¼	550	3¾	2.1		
1½	700	4	2.3		
2	900	5	2.8		
3	1.4 kg	6	3.4		
4	1.8	7	4.0		
5	2.3	8 (1 gal.)	4.5		

Note: All the recipes in this book will serve 4–6 people, according to appetite.

SUMPTUOUS
SOUPS

There is infinite pleasure to be had in making a soup that is both satisfying to eat and nourishing as well. The basis of a good soup – as indeed of all cooking – is good produce, but the real foundation is a rich stock that can be made with a left-over carcase or joint bone. A simple chicken stock is probably one of the most widely used.

CHICKEN STOCK

1 cooked chicken carcase	*1 tsp mixed herbs (or use fresh ones)*
1 onion	*Salt and black pepper*
1 large carrot	*Water to cover*
4 sticks celery	

Break up the carcase in a large pan, cut up the vegetables, and sprinkle over the herbs, salt and pepper. Cover with water and bring to the boil. Allow to simmer for 1½ hours. Strain through a colander, and then allow the stock to go cold before removing any excess fat.

You can always vary the ingredients for your basic stock a little, according to taste. Try adding one or two cloves of garlic and a bay leaf. Fresh herbs make a delicious difference. If you wish to be really professional, then use an uncooked bird and make a larger quantity of stock: you will find that it will set like a jelly.

Stock for game is made in a similar way using the broken-up carcases of pheasant or other game birds, but benefits from the addition of some strong flavours like a slice of gammon and a blade of mace.

Fish stock is probably the one people tend to make least, perhaps because it can sometimes be a bit difficult getting hold of fish bones. But it is well worth going to the trouble of doing so, even if it may seem a bit extravagant to use whole fish simply to make a stock. Never use oily fish like herring or mackerel. Skate and plaice bones are probably the best. Wash the bones thoroughly and prepare the stock in the same way as the chicken stock with the addition of some stalks of parsley or parsley roots. If you would like a brown fish stock, then brown all the bones and the vegetables in a little butter first.

It is well worth the labour of making a vegetable stock – the results can be surprisingly rewarding.

VEGETABLE STOCK

1 large onion	1 leek
3 potatoes	1½ oz butter
3 carrots	3 pints water
2 turnips	Salt
4 sticks celery	

Wash, peel and chop up all the vegetables and fry them in the butter. Cover with boiling water, add salt to taste and simmer for a couple of hours. Strain the stock, and it is ready for use.

If you have a small kitchen and the thought of having a pan simmering away on top of the stove for hours is offputting, then there is an alternative method. Add boiling water to all your stock ingredients, put the whole lot in a casserole, and simply pop it in a medium-hot oven to simmer away. In a couple of hours you will have a delicious stock which can be used not only for soups but of course for gravies and in pie fillings as well. It is a good idea to make stock in large quantities to put in the freezer. If you pour it into a number of small containers for freezing, then you can simply use it as required.

The art of making soup is really like that of making a fine wine – the skill lies in subtly blending the flavours of the different ingredients together. Like an apéritif, it should satisfy in itself, as well as entice you on to the next course. The recipe suggestions I offer below are only a very small sample of the combinations of flavours and textures you can try. Experiment with your own variations and additions to the basic themes I give – and remember: the better the quality of the ingredients you use, the better the taste. But not all need be expensive – indeed, some may even be had for nothing, as in the tasty and interesting recipe for Nettle Soup that follows.

NETTLE SOUP

A panful of young nettles	2 oz plain flour
¼ pint water	1 pint chicken stock (see p. 10)
1 small onion, chopped	Salt and pepper to season
2 oz butter	1 tbsp soured cream

Take great care how you collect the young nettles – be sure to wear gloves! Wash them well and press them down into a large saucepan. Add the onion and the water, cover and simmer for about 15 minutes. Strain the nettles and liquidise in a food processor.

In a thick saucepan melt the butter and add the flour and cook for a minute. Stir in the chicken stock and bring to the boil. Cook for a few minutes, then stir in the nettles and heat through. Just before serving adjust the seasoning and stir in the soured cream.

PEA SOUP

1 lb fresh peas (shelled weight)	1½ pints water
1 bunch spring onions, chopped	1 rounded tsp sugar
1 bunch watercress, chopped	1 tbsp cream
1 sprig mint, chopped	4 oz unsalted butter

Place the spring onions, watercress and mint in a pan. Add the freshly shelled peas, cover with the water and simmer for about 20 minutes. Stir in the sugar and cream, then pour the soup into a food processor with the butter and liquidise. Warm the soup through and serve with a swirl of cream.

COURGETTE SOUP

1 lb courgettes	2 oz butter
½ pint milk	1 medium onion, sliced
½ lb potatoes, cubed	Salt and black pepper
1 pint vegetable stock	

Slice the courgettes into a thick saucepan, add a little salt and cover with the milk. Simmer gently until the courgettes are soft. Add the potato cubes to the vegetable stock and season with a little salt. Allow the potatoes to cook in the vegetable stock (7–10 minutes).

Melt the butter in a frying pan and gently sauté the sliced onion until cooked but not brown.

Strain the juices from the courgettes and the potatoes and put on one side. Blend together the potatoes, courgettes and onions in a food processor or liquidiser until you have a smooth paste. Add to the reserved stock/milk mixture in a pan and heat through gently, stirring continually. Adjust the seasoning and serve.

TOMATO SOUP

2 lb tomatoes	1 dsp basil, chopped
2 onions, finely chopped	4 pints water
2 carrots, finely chopped	Juice of 1 lemon
2 sticks celery, finely chopped	1 tsp sugar
2 oz butter	1 oz vermicelli
2 oz cornflour	Salt and black pepper
1 tbsp parsley, chopped	Single cream to garnish

The first – and worst – job is to skin and deseed the tomatoes. (It is a mistake to use tomatoes that are already past their best!) If you have a gas cooker, spear the tomatoes with a long-handled fork and turn them over a high flame for a second or two before removing the skins. They should come away quite easily. Otherwise drop them one or two at a time into a pan of boiling water. Fish them out with a tea strainer and, when cool enough to handle, pull the skins away. Cut them in quarters and remove the seeds. It's better to be generous than mean with the number of tomatoes you use.

Put the onions, carrots and celery in a large, thick saucepan with the butter and cook until they are softened but do not allow them to brown. Add the tomatoes and cook for a further 5 minutes. Sprinkle on the cornflour and add the chopped herbs. Cook for a further minute.

Gently stir in the water and lemon juice, and allow the whole lot to simmer for about 20 minutes before adding the sugar and vermicelli and seasoning with salt and pepper. Cover with a close-fitting lid and simmer for a further 10 minutes.

If you wish, liquidise the soup in a food processor before heating. Serve in warmed soup plates. I like to spoon a tablespoon of single cream into the *bottom* of each soup plate just before serving. Croutons are an added luxury.

SPRING VEGETABLE SOUP

4 oz fresh shelled peas	1 oz butter
6 asparagus spears	1 pint milk
6 spring onions	5 fl oz single cream
2 small carrots	Salt and black pepper

Wash all the vegetables and cut them up where necessary. Melt the butter in a thick saucepan and add the vegetables, cover the pan tightly, and cook gently until the vegetables are soft but not brown – keep shaking the pan across the heat to avoid browning them.

Add the milk and cream and simmer for 15 minutes. Adjust the seasoning and serve.

BAKED POTATO SOUP

3 baked potatoes	1 egg yolk
3 tbsp hot milk	5 fl oz cream
1 small onion, sliced	Salt and pepper
2 pints well-seasoned chicken stock	1 tbsp freshly chopped parsley

Split the baked potatoes and remove the insides but do not discard the shells (see p. 23 for what to do with those). Whip the potato with the hot milk.

Sauté the sliced onion in a little butter in a pan and cook until it is soft. Add the potato and onion to the stock. Beat the egg yolk, add a little of the stock and beat again until smooth. Then add the cream before stirring the mixture into the rest of the stock. Gently heat the soup through but do not let it boil. Adjust the seasoning and serve sprinkled with fresh parsley.

KIDNEY SOUP

12 oz lamb's kidneys	Sprig of parsley
1 small onion, finely chopped	Salt and black pepper
2 oz unsalted butter	1 wineglass port
1 oz plain flour	Croutons to garnish
1½ pints chicken stock	

Dice the cored and washed kidneys. Melt the butter in a thick saucepan and fry the chopped onion and the kidney for a few minutes, making sure you keep stirring all the time so as not to harden the meat. Sprinkle on the flour and add the stock. Bring to the boil, add the sprig of parsley and simmer until smooth and thick. Check the seasoning and allow to simmer for another 30 minutes. Stir in the glass of port 5 minutes before serving and heat through again. Sprinkle each helping with freshly made croutons.

ST HUBERT'S GROUSE SOUP

4 oz orange lentils	4 oz butter
1 brace grouse	Sprig thyme
4 rashers smoked back bacon	1 bay leaf
2 carrots, diced	1 onion, chopped
2 shallots, chopped	2½ pints water
2 sticks celery, sliced	2 oz rice
1 leek, sliced	Salt and black pepper
4 oz smoked bacon, diced	Crisply fried bacon cubes to garnish

Soak the lentils in water for a couple of hours.

Wrap each grouse in 2 rashers of back bacon and roast in a very hot oven, gas mark 7, 425°F (220°C), for about 18 minutes.

Put the prepared vegetables (the carrots, shallots, celery and leek) along with the smoked bacon, the sprig of thyme and the bay leaf in a small, thick casserole and cook very gently in 1 ounce of butter until they are just softened and not mushy.

Remove the flesh from the breasts and legs of the roast grouse. Place the carcases in a large pan along with the meat, the onion and the rest of the butter. Cover with the water and boil until the liquid has reduced by about one quarter.

Strain the stock into another large pan to which you have already added the cooked vegetables and bacon. Strain the lentils and add these to the pan along with the rice. Simmer for about an hour, then pass the mixture through a food processor.

Check the seasoning before heating and serve with the crisply fried bacon cubes sprinkled on top.

CRAB SOUP

1 tbsp butter	1 pint milk
½ small onion, grated	¼ pint cream
8 oz cooked crab meat	Salt and black pepper
¼ tsp curry powder	1 tbsp dry sherry

Melt the butter in a thick saucepan and add the grated onion. Cook very gently until the onion is soft, remove from the heat and stir in the crab meat. Heat through, add the curry powder, milk and cream. Season with salt and pepper, and just before serving add the sherry.

This is a very rich soup and is best served with a simple dish to follow. It can be made with lobster if the family budget stretches to it!

FISH CHOWDER

1 onion, chopped	1½ pints milk
2 carrots, diced	12 oz fresh white fish (haddock or cod)
2 sticks celery, sliced	4 oz prawns
1 lb potatoes, diced	½ oz cornflour
4 oz streaky bacon, diced	Juice of 1 lemon
1 oz unsalted butter	Single cream for garnish
Salt and pepper	1 tbsp chopped parsley

Fry the vegetables and bacon in the melted butter. Season with some salt and pepper and cook for about 6 minutes. Stir in 1 pint of the milk and simmer for 10 minutes.

Cut the fish up into small chunks and add them with the prawns to the soup. Make sure that this is simmering gently as you do not want to break up the vegetables.

Blend the cornflour with the remaining milk, stir into the pan and gently bring the soup to the boil until it begins to thicken. Add the lemon juice and adjust the seasoning.

Stir a tablespoon of single cream into each dish and sprinkle each helping with chopped parsley just before serving.

STARTER'S
ORDERS

It never takes long to finish a meal, but it often takes ages to get started! Starters hint at tempting things to come so you need to choose something that will excite and stimulate the appetite, but not overwhelm the rest of the meal. Don't serve something with a dominating flavour – such as garlic, or lemon – if you are planning to repeat the flavour later on, or if the succeeding dish will contrast harshly with it. Try and find subtle and interesting contrasts – and try and vary the texture of your dishes too. A bland mousse followed by a dish cooked in a smooth white sauce will make the meal a bit boring: it would have been better to open proceedings with a crisp, chewy starter such as Mussels in Garlic Butter or a salad of some sort. I always think it's a good idea to use the first course as the chance to experiment with a new recipe that you are considering serving as a main course on a later occasion. If your guests leave most of it on their plates, then you'll get the message!

I didn't realise until I sat down to list the starters in this chapter that so many of my favourites come out of the sea. East Anglia, where I was brought up, is surrounded by sea and it is probably because of those lingering memories of superb mussels from Felixstowe, crabs from Cromer and sprats from Great Yarmouth that I have drawn so heavily on them.

CHEESE SOUFFLÉS

4 oz old potatoes	2 egg whites
1 oz butter	2 oz farmhouse cheddar, finely grated
1 egg yolk	

For this you will need 4 small ramekins. Take half the butter and grease the ramekins well.

Boil the potatoes and mash them while they are still warm, adding the rest of the butter to them. Beat the egg yolk well, add this to the potatoes and mix well in.

Beat the egg whites until they peak and fold them into the potato mixture before lightly adding the finely-grated cheese. (If you put the cheese in the coolest part of the fridge for an hour first, then you should have no difficulty in grating it finely without it crumbling.)

Pour the mixture equally into the greased ramekins. If you have very small ones, then you may need to make greaseproof paper collars for them since the soufflés will rise. Put the ramekins in the oven at gas mark 5, 375°F (190°C) for 20 minutes. Serve immediately.

BACON AND MUSHROOM STARTER

4 oz fresh button mushrooms	*1 oz butter*
4 oz green streaky or back bacon	*Black pepper*
4 circles of fresh bread (see recipe)	*1 tbsp chopped parsley*
2 oz lard or oil	

If possible, you'll need two or three frying pans ready to achieve the best results, and have the ingredients prepared before you start cooking. Slice the mushrooms very carefully. Make sure they are *really* fresh – if you can't get fresh button ones, then don't bother to try the dish. Cut up the bacon into small strips.

Using a small saucer as a template, cut out circles of freshly-made, thick-sliced bread. Melt the lard or oil in a fairly large frying pan until it will quickly brown a cube of bread. Add the bread circles and brown them quickly on both sides. Place them on a wire rack in the oven to keep warm.

Melt the butter in a small frying pan and add the mushrooms and cook quickly. At the same time cook the bacon strips until they are crisp and then add them to the mushrooms. Twist on a good deal of black pepper.

Place each of the fried-bread croutons on a warmed plate and pile on equal portions of the mushroom and bacon. Sprinkle with fresh parsley and serve piping hot.

This mouthwatering, yet simple, starter is one that never fails to get the gastric juices running.

HAM AND FRESH FIGS

8 fresh figs	*8 slices of thinly sliced ham*

Wash the figs and wrap them in the ham. Place on a dish in the fridge to chill well. A delicious way to start a summer feast.

MUSHROOM PÂTÉ

4 oz onion, chopped	¼ tsp ground nutmeg
12 oz field mushrooms, sliced	2 fl oz Marsala
4 oz unsalted butter	4 oz soured cream
Black pepper	

Gently fry the finely chopped onion in 2 ounces of the butter. Add the sliced mushrooms and the black pepper and nutmeg, and continue to cook gently until soft.

Pour the Marsala over the mixture and cook for another 3 minutes. When cool, purée the mixture in a food processor with the rest of the butter and the soured cream. Spoon into ramekins, chill and serve.

SIMPLE SIMON'S SMOKED FISH PÂTÉ

¾ lb smoked fish	Juice and rind of 1 lemon
Freshly ground black pepper	¼ pint soured cream
Grated nutmeg	

Poach the fish in a little milk with black pepper. Remove the skin and bones. Flake the flesh into a bowl. Grate on some black pepper and add the grated nutmeg with the grated rind and juice of the lemon. Fold in the soured cream. Chill.

SALMON MOUSSE

3 tsp powdered gelatine	1 lb cooked salmon, flaked
¼ pint vinegar and water, mixed	½ stick celery, finely chopped
1 tsp salt	1 tbsp horseradish sauce
1 tsp sugar	1 tsp freshly made mustard
5 fl oz double cream	Watercress to decorate

Soak the gelatine in the vinegar and water and then dissolve by heating in a warm pan of water. Add the salt and the sugar. Whip the double cream and blend with the gelatine mixture. Fork in the flaked salmon and the finely chopped celery with the horseradish sauce and the mustard. Pour into a mould and chill well until set. Serve on a bed of watercress.

HERRING POTS

6 herrings	1/2 tsp ground nutmeg
1/2 pint apple juice	Salt and black pepper
6 oz unsalted butter	Melted butter to seal
2 oz soured cream	

Wash and clean the herrings and place in an ovenproof dish. Cover with the apple juice and cook in the oven at gas mark 5, 375°F (190°C) for 30 minutes.

When cool, remove the skin and bone from the fish and place the flesh in a bowl. Mash with the butter and soured cream (melt the butter very gently over a saucepan of boiling water if it is very hard). Add the nutmeg and seasoning, making sure the mixture is well blended.

Spoon into ramekins and cover with some melted butter. Chill for an hour or two and serve.

POTTED CRAB

2 egg yolks	1 lb cooked crab meat
3 tbsp soured cream	Pinch cayenne pepper
Salt and black pepper	Melted butter to seal
2 oz unsalted butter	

Mix the egg yolks and the cream together with the salt and black pepper. Melt the butter in a thick saucepan and add the cooked crab meat, mashing it into the butter, and heat through. Stir into the cream mixture and place the bowl in a pan of lightly simmering water over a low heat: stir continually until the mixture thickens.

Spoon the mixture into small ramekins, scatter with cayenne pepper and pour some melted butter on the top. Allow to chill. Serve with crisp wholemeal bread.

SPRAT FLATS

12 oz puff pastry	1 tsp fresh basil, chopped
½ oz butter	A sprig of thyme
1 small onion, chopped	Salt and black pepper
1 clove garlic, chopped	16 sprats
1 tin chopped tomatoes	

Set the oven to gas mark 6, 400°F (200°C). Roll the puff pastry out into a rectangle large enough to cut 4 saucer-sized discs from. Place the circles of pastry on a baking tray and cook in the oven for 10 minutes.

In a frying pan melt the butter and add the chopped onion and garlic. Cook until they are just beginning to brown. Add the tin of chopped tomato, the herbs and seasoning, and heat through.

Spread each pastry round with a little of the tomato sauce and arrange 4 sprats on the top of each one. Return to the oven and cook for a further 15 minutes.

Serve immediately. This is an unusual and tasty starter.

FISH KEBABS

4 oz haddock	8 bay leaves
4 oz cod	Black pepper
4 oz rock salmon	2 tbsp unsalted butter, melted
8 mussels	1 small lettuce
8 button mushrooms	1 wineglassful of brandy
4 tomatoes, halved	

Cut the fish into small chunks. Remove the uncooked mussels from their shells with a sharp knife. Thread onto 4 skewers alternately with the mushrooms, tomatoes and bay leaves. Sprinkle the fish with lots of black pepper and coat each skewer liberally with the melted butter.

Turn the grill on high and gradually cook the fish for about 10 minutes, basting from time to time with any spare melted butter.

In the meantime shred the lettuce and divide between 4 plates.

When the fish is almost cooked pour the brandy over the skewers and set light to them, serving immediately on a bed of lettuce.

MUSSELS IN GARLIC BUTTER

3 dozen large fresh mussels	4 tbsp chopped parsley
6 oz unsalted butter	Pinch of nutmeg
2 oz shallots, chopped	Salt and pepper
6 cloves garlic	

Wash and scrub the mussels. Reject any which are cracked or open. In a food processor blend together all the rest of the ingredients to make the garlic butter. Place a knob of butter upon each mussel and pop them under a fierce grill until the butter bubbles.

Serve with fresh French bread.

FISH AND AVOCADO LONG BOATS

4 half shells from 2 baked potatoes	1 oz butter
8 oz white fish	1 oz flour
4 oz smoked fish	Salt and black pepper
½ pint milk	Chopped flesh of 2 avocados
1 bay leaf	Chopped parsley to garnish

Here's what to do with the potato skins you reserved from the Baked Potato Soup (see p. 14).

Heat the oil in a deep fat fryer to a temperature for making chips and deep fry each of the potato shells until it is really crispy but not burnt. Remove from the oil, keep warm, and allow to drain on kitchen paper.

For the filling, gently poach all the fish in the milk with the bay leaf. Reserve the resulting stock and proceed to skin and flake the fish. In a thick saucepan melt the butter and add the flour, allowing to cook for a minute or two before adding the fishy milk to make a white sauce. Season as necessary.

At the bottom of each of the potato shells place a little chopped up avocado. Mix the flaked fish into the white sauce and pour on top of the avocado in the potato shells.

Sprinkle with parsley and serve immediately.

GAME PÂTÉ

½ lb streaky bacon rashers	2 pigeon breasts
1 small onion, finely chopped	¼ lb pig's liver
1 oz unsalted butter	¼ lb smoked gammon
1 clove garlic, chopped	¼ tsp ground nutmeg
6 juniper berries, crushed	1 tsp mixed herbs
1 small rabbit, jointed and boned	1 glass port

Set the oven to gas mark 2, 300°F (150°C). Line a 1-pint terrine with the streaky bacon.

Soften the finely chopped onion in the butter and add the chopped garlic and the crushed juniper berries. Fry for 1 minute.

Coarsely mince the rabbit, pigeon breasts, liver and gammon together. Add the onion mixture, with nutmeg and herbs and the glass of port. Mix well together and spoon into the prepared terrine. Cover with a tight-fitting lid and stand in a dish of water. Bake in the oven for 3 hours.

Chill well and serve garnished with pickled gherkins.

TERRINE OF CHICKEN BREAST

1 lb uncooked chicken meat	8 oz broccoli spears
3 egg whites	4 oz carrots, cut in matchsticks
Salt and pepper	3 large, whole field mushrooms
2 tsp powdered gelatine	2 oz butter
½ pint double cream	1 small lettuce, chopped

Place the chicken and egg whites in a food processor and season with some salt and pepper. Process until you have a smooth paste. Pour into a bowl, cover, and chill well.

Gently heat 2 tablespoons of water in a cup and add the gelatine until it has dissolved. Blend with the double cream and add to the chicken mixture.

Cook the broccoli spears for 4 minutes in salted boiling water. Drain and purée in a food processor. Cook the carrot matchsticks in salted boiling water for 4 minutes. Fry the whole mushrooms gently in butter for 2 minutes, making sure they remain firm.

Butter a 9-inch soufflé dish. Place one of the mushrooms at the bottom of the dish and arrange one-third of the carrot matchsticks to fill up the space around. Spoon a layer of the well-chilled chicken mixture over, then add a layer of broccoli purée and some more chicken. Place on this the second mushroom with some more carrot matchsticks, followed by the layers of chicken and broccoli, then repeat everything one more time.

Cover the top with some greased foil. Place in a bain-marie in the oven at gas mark 4, 350°F (180°C) for 45 minutes. Allow to cool, then chill well. Stand the mould in a bowl of warm water and turn out onto a bed of chopped lettuce.

NO ORDINARY
PORK TERRINE

8 oz streaky bacon rashers	2 large eggs, beaten
2 lb piece belly pork	1 sprig each rosemary, thyme, basil
8 oz smoked gammon	and marjoram
8 oz pig's liver	1 tsp ground mace
2 large onions	2 large field mushrooms, sliced
2 cloves garlic	2 large chicken breasts, cooked
10 juniper berries	

Line a very large terrine or oval casserole with the rashers of streaky bacon. Set the oven to gas mark 2, 300°F (150°C).

Coarsely mince the belly pork, gammon, liver, onions, garlic and juniper berries. Add the eggs with the herbs and mace and mix well in. Place one quarter of this mixture in the bottom of the prepared terrine and place one of the sliced mushrooms on top. Cover with some more of the mixture and then lay the 2 cooked chicken breasts in the middle. Add a little more of the mixture, then the other sliced mushroom, before topping up with the rest of the mixture.

Cover the terrine with a firm-fitting lid and place in a bowl of boiling water. Put in the oven for 1½ hours, or until it is beginning to come away from the side of the dish. Remove and chill. Serve with fresh brown bread.

A KETTLE OF FISH

The Scottish salmon industry has grown enormously over the last fifteen years: salmon farms are now found all along the west coast, into the Highlands and the Hebrides. A good deal of fresh salmon is exported to France and at least one Scottish fish farmer has a Canadian Government licence to supply smolts (young fish) to Canada. Sixty per cent of the 6000 tons of farmed salmon produced in 1985 went for smoking, and the market for this luxury item is so large that a lot of fish is imported into this country specially for smoking. (Read the label – if it says Scottish Smoked Salmon it may well be imported salmon that has been smoked in Scotland, but if it says Smoked Scottish Salmon it is the real thing.) All this means that salmon is now widely available in most fishmongers, and although it still remains an expensive item, it is cheaper than some cuts of beef. (The recipe for Salmon Pie that I have included is well worth noting, since it does make a little go a long way.) Yet I'm afraid that a lot of the snobbery attached to salmon lingers on.

The basic ingredients of the other fish dishes I've included have always had a much humbler place in our nation's diet. Indeed, oysters were traditionally poor man's food that London cockneys added to steak and kidney pie to eke out the meat. Colchester oysters are delicious. Try them in the recipe for Oyster Fries if you cannot bear the idea of eating a raw oyster. They are far meatier and tastier than many French oysters, in my opinion.

Kippers and bloaters, too, were a traditional way of preserving the herring catch for winter eating, and smokeries existed all round our coasts. Many people consider Loch Fyne kippers the sweetest and tastiest of all, and Arbroath smokies are another local Scottish speciality – you can use Yarmouth bloaters if you cannot obtain the genuine article.

It is an indication of how much the food industry is expanding that experiments are now being carried out to try and grow mussels on strings off piers in the sea. As children we used to pluck them from the long concrete and wooden breakers that reach out into the sea at Felixstowe in Suffolk; although often quite small, they were delicious. Coupled with some good Suffolk cider they are unique.

SALMON PIE

12 oz fresh salmon	2 tbsp double cream
1 pint milk	6 oz button mushrooms
1 bay leaf	12 oz puff pastry
Salt and black pepper	1 beaten egg for glazing
1 oz cornflour	

Cut the fresh salmon into chunks about 1 inch square, and add to a thick saucepan with the milk, bay leaf and a little black pepper and salt. Gently bring the milk to the boil and then turn off immediately and leave to cool.

Strain off the milk into another pan, stir in the cornflour and allow to thicken over a gentle heat. Remove the sauce from the heat and stir in the double cream.

Line a large, 1½-pint pie dish with pastry and arrange the salmon chunks and the mushrooms inside. Pour the sauce over and cover with a pastry lid. Seal well down and glaze with the beaten egg.

Bake in the oven at gas mark 7, 425°F (220°C) for about 10 minutes, and then turn the oven down to gas mark 5, 375°F (190°C) for another 15 minutes.

Serve this delicious pie with some minted new potatoes and fresh broad beans. It really is delicious, and a good way of making a little salmon go a long way. The filling itself can be served in various other ways – with rice or noodles, or any other form of pasta. A few walnuts sprinkled on the top lifts it into another dimension.

BAKED SALMON JOINT

1 × 2 lb middle cut salmon joint	6 oz mushrooms, thinly sliced
3 oz unsalted butter	1 oz fresh dill, finely chopped
Freshly ground black pepper	1 wineglass dry sherry
Juice of 2 lemons	8 fl oz cream

Ask your fishmonger to reserve a centre portion of a salmon for you to cook as a joint – he may not be used to the idea at the moment but it is catching on rapidly. Make sure the fish has been well cleaned out so that there are no dark patches of blood.

Preheat the oven to gas mark 5, 375°F (190°C). Place the joint in an oven dish and dot with butter. Sprinkle liberally with freshly ground black pepper and squeeze on the lemon juice. Cover loosely with kitchen foil and cook in the oven for 25 minutes. Remove the joint from the oven dish and cover with the foil to keep warm while you prepare the sauce.

Over a low flame add the mushrooms and dill to the juices in the oven dish and allow to cook gently. When the mushrooms are cooked, gently pour on the sherry and allow the juices to reduce a little over a rapid flame. Finally, remove the pan from the heat and allow to stand for 1 minute before adding the cream. Return to the heat and bring to a very gentle simmer. Pour the sauce onto a preheated meat dish and place the salmon joint majestically in the middle.

MARINATED SCOTTISH SALMON with Mustard Sauce

2 lb Scottish salmon	4 tbsp sugar
2 tsp olive oil	2 tsp crushed peppercorns
4 tbsp coarse salt	Masses of fresh dill
FOR THE SAUCE	
4 oz butter	1 level tbsp English mustard
1 oz flour	1 tbsp tarragon vinegar
¾ pint milk	1 level tsp sugar
Salt and pepper	1 level tsp chopped fresh dill

Scrape the scales off the fish and fillet it (or ask your fishmonger to do this for you). Turn the fish over in the oil and rub the salt, sugar and crushed peppercorns into the flesh.

Place handfuls of freshly washed dill on the bottom of a shallow dish and place one piece of the salmon, flesh side down, on top. Place the other piece on top, flesh side up, and cover with more dill. Put a flat plate with a heavy weight on the top of it and place in the fridge for about 5 days, keeping the fish lightly covered.

Slice the fish into chunks and serve with the mustard sauce. To make this, melt the butter in a thick saucepan and blend in the flour and milk to make a white sauce. Cook for 2 minutes. Season with salt and pepper and stir in the rest of the ingredients. Cover with a piece of wet greaseproof paper, and allow to cool.

STUFFED SALMON TROUT

1 large salmon trout	Black pepper
2 oz butter	

FOR THE STUFFING

8 oz whiting	¼ pint soured cream
2 small egg whites	1 lime

Preheat the oven to gas mark 4, 350°F (180°C).

Make sure the salmon trout is well cleaned. Lay it on a large baking dish and dot the inside with the butter and freshly ground black pepper.

To make the stuffing, skin the whiting and mince it coarsely. Fold in the beaten egg whites. Mix in the soured cream and add the juice and finely grated rind of the lime.

Place the stuffing inside the fish and reshape. Bake in the oven for 25 minutes. Serve with freshly boiled new potatoes.

BAKED TROUT with Prune Sauce

4 trout	Black pepper
2 oz unsalted butter	Juice of 2 lemons
Fresh tarragon	

FOR THE SAUCE

1 small onion, finely chopped	1 tbsp tarragon vinegar
1 oz unsalted butter	1 tbsp soured cream
6 oz cooked prunes, stones removed	

If you are at all squeamish, ask your fishmonger to gut and clean the fish for you, making especially sure that there is no evidence of blood along the backbone.

Preheat the oven to gas mark 5, 375°F (190°C). Place the trout in a baking dish which has been buttered with 1 ounce of butter. Inside each of the cleaned fish place a sprig of fresh tarragon and a little freshly ground black pepper. Dot the rest of the butter over the trout, and sprinkle with the lemon juice. Cover loosely with a piece of foil and bake in the oven for about 15 minutes. If the dorsal fin is easily removed when lifted between finger and thumb, then you'll know that the fish is cooked to perfection.

Whilst the trout is cooking, prepare the sauce. Finely chop the onion and cook it very gently in a thick saucepan with the butter, without browning. Add the prunes and heat through. Place these ingredients in a food processor with a tablespoon of tarragon vinegar, and blend until smooth. Finally add the soured cream and blend for a second or two longer.

Remove the fish from the oven and serve on hot plates with a spoonful of the sauce.

A delicious variation of the sauce can be made with fresh damsons.

KINNOULL SMOKIE SUPPER

1 lb Arbroath smokies (or bloaters or kippers)	3 tomatoes, skinned, deseeded and chopped
1 pint milk	1½ oz flour
2 oz butter	2 oz cheddar cheese, grated
2 onions, chopped	Pepper
4 rashers smoked bacon, diced	Paprika to garnish

Cover the fish with milk in a large saucepan and gently bring to the boil for about a minute. Drain the fish, reserving the milk, and remove the skin and bones. Put the fish on one side. Preheat the oven to gas mark 5, 375°F (190°C).

Melt 1 ounce of butter and gently fry the chopped onion and bacon together. When the onion is soft add the tomatoes and cook for a further minute.

In a small saucepan melt the remaining ounce of butter and add the flour and the milk reserved from cooking the fish to make a white sauce. When the sauce begins to boil, stir in the grated cheese, and add some pepper but *no* salt as the salt in the fish and the bacon will be enough.

Place the pieces of fish in a buttered baking dish and cover with the bacon, onion and tomato mixture. Pour over the cheese sauce and sprinkle a little paprika over the top. Heat through in the centre of the oven for half an hour.

Alternatively, you can make this recipe in small ramekins (the cooking time will be slightly shorter) and serve as an unusual starter.

KIPPERS WITH MUSHROOMS

1 brace Loch Fyne kippers	4 oz button mushrooms, finely sliced

Ideally, this dish should be made in a steamer, but if you do not have one, try cooking it between two plates with a bit of butter over a saucepan of boiling water.

Place the kippers on the rack of the steamer, and pile the finely sliced mushrooms on top. Steam for about 12 minutes. Serve immediately with some fresh brown bread and butter.

The joy of this delicious recipe – which was given to me by a friend, Jeff Edge, who (he'll forgive me saying) has to watch his weight – is that it is so simple to prepare, and *good for you*, being low in calories.

SMOKED HADDOCK SOUFFLÉ

1½ oz unsalted butter	½ pint milk
1 tsp dried sage (or 1 level dsp if fresh)	1 bay leaf
	1 oz plain flour
6 oz smoked haddock	4 eggs, separated

You will need a 2-pint soufflé dish for the quantities given here. Rub ½ ounce of butter round the dish, and then toss in the sage, shaking it all around to cover the floor and walls of the dish.

Place the smoked haddock and milk in a shallow oven dish with the bay leaf and cook in the oven at gas mark 5, 375°F (190°C) for about 15 minutes. Remove the fish for flaking, and reserve the milk. Raise the temperature of the oven to gas mark 8, 450°F (230°C).

In a large saucepan, and it really does need to be large, melt the rest of the butter and stir in the flour and then the milk, stirring all the time until you have a fairly smooth paste. Remove from the heat and beat in the egg yolks one at a time, making sure they are well blended. If you have problems at this point now is the time to put them right. If the mixture goes lumpy or the eggs are not blended well enough, then reach for the food processor and pour everything in and give it a second or two to blend – a marvellous rescue operation, this. Return the mixture to the pan.

Beat the egg whites until they are really stiff and standing in firm peaks. Fold them into the sauce, and then add the flaked fish. Be careful in the folding-in process that you do not knock all the air out of the egg whites.

Immediately place the dish in the preheated oven, and leave for about 25 minutes. There is nothing you can do now, so sit back, relax, and forget about it. When you open the oven door, the soufflé should be puffy and well risen, with a delicious brown crust.

Serve immediately with a crisp green salad.

OYSTER FRIES

24 Colchester oysters	1 tbsp finely chopped parsley
1 lb cooked fresh prawns	Oil for deep frying
2 oz unsalted butter	Juice of 2 lemons
5 fl oz single cream	
FOR THE BATTER	
4 oz plain flour	¼ pint milk
1 egg	Salt

Wash and clean the oysters well. Remove them from their shells with a strong-bladed knife, making sure you reserve all their natural juice. Place them with the juice in a large, thick saucepan and cook gently for about 3 minutes. Remove and drain well. Remove the cooked prawns from their shells.

Make up the batter in the usual way. I use the all-in-one method in a food processor, which seems to work quite well, and allow the batter to stand for about half an hour in a cool place.

In the meantime, melt the butter in another large, thick saucepan. Stir in the prawns and allow to heat through. Stir in the cream. Place the prawns on the bottom of a shallow dish and sprinkle well with freshly chopped parsley. Keep warm.

Heat the oil to the correct temperature for deep frying. Quickly dip each oyster in the batter and deep fry until the batter is crispy. (If you have a deep-frying basket, you can do several at a time.)

Place the oysters on top of the prawns and sprinkle well with lemon juice. Serve immediately.

MUSSELS IN SUFFOLK CIDER

2 quarts mussels	2 tbsp chopped parsley
½ pint strong dry cider	Black pepper
10 spring onions, chopped	1 oz unsalted butter

Scrub the mussels and throw away any that are open. Remove any beards that show. Place the mussels in a large pan and pour on the cider. Add the chopped spring onions and parsley, and grind over some black pepper. Cover and bring to the boil. Simmer for 15 minutes, shaking the pan occasionally, until the shells are open (discard any that fail to open). Drop the butter on the mussels and shake the pan.

Divide the mussels between your guests and serve with fresh bread rolls. Don't forget a large bowl for the empty shells, and lots of napkins too!

FOWL
PLAY

In the old days, of course, a plump roasted fowl was a real treat on the family table, marking a high day or special celebration. Now poultry – especially chicken – has a major place in our national diet, particularly as the red, fattier meats have fallen, to some extent, into disfavour. More of that later! I've collected chicken recipes from all over the country which show how much of a favourite it has become, and the growing choice of chickens and other fowl available to us reflects the demand that shoppers are influencing over suppliers. Thank goodness we no longer have to make do only with pallid, flavourless, frozen chickens. Chilled chicken – so much more tender and full of taste – is one product that is appearing more and more widely; another is 'corn-fed' chicken. These have a slightly yellow colour to their skin since – as their name suggests – they have been fed on maize. Try them – they are delicious. Look out, too, for those boneless duck breasts in many supermarkets. They make an interesting change, and really do save you a lot of bother. And talking of changes, why don't you try a goose this year for Christmas dinner? They always used to be the traditional dish in all parts of the country, fattened up in country orchards on fallen apples during the autumn months.

Roast chicken is still a firm favourite of mine, especially at Sunday lunchtime. I simply rub the skin with oil and salt, place an onion in the body cavity, and roast it in the oven. But you can ring all sorts of changes with different stuffings, and so I have begun this section with a number of suggested stuffings for poultry of all kinds.

FOUR STUFFINGS

VEAL AND HAM STUFFING for turkey	
4 oz lean veal	4 oz fresh breadcrumbs
4 oz gammon steak	1 tbsp chopped parsley
1 small onion, grated	1/2 tsp nutmeg
1 oz unsalted butter	1 beaten egg

Mince the veal and gammon coarsely together. Fry the grated onion in the melted butter until it is soft. Mix with all the other ingredients and stuff into the cavity of the bird. Use double this quantity if you have a very large turkey.

APPLE AND CELERY STUFFING

1 oz unsalted butter	4 oz breadcrumbs
4 oz smoked bacon, chopped	2 tbsp chopped parsley
8 oz onion, chopped	1 dsp demerara sugar
2 sticks celery, chopped	10 crushed coriander seeds
4 oz cooking apples, sliced	

Melt the butter in a frying pan, and cook the finely chopped bacon, onion and celery for 5 minutes. Add the apples and cook for a further 3 minutes. Mix with all the other ingredients, and stuff into the cavity of the bird.

This stuffing is excellent with all kinds of poultry.

NUT STUFFING for turkey

2 oz butter	4 oz walnuts, chopped
2 small onions, finely chopped	6 oz fresh breadcrumbs
6 oz mushrooms, sliced	1 tbsp chopped parsley
4 oz hazelnuts, chopped	½ tsp mixed herbs
4 oz brazil nuts, chopped	1 large egg
4 oz almonds, chopped	

Melt the butter and gently fry the onions and the mushrooms until soft. Mix together with all the other ingredients, and bind with the egg. Set aside to get firm before stuffing the bird.

APRICOT AND TANGERINE STUFFING for duck

2 oz unsalted butter	8 oz fresh breadcrumbs
2 onions, finely chopped	2 oz hazelnuts, chopped
1 tsp curry powder	1 tsp salt
6 oz dried apricots	1 beaten egg
2 tangerines	

Melt the butter in a frying pan and gently fry the onions. Add the curry powder and cook for 2 minutes more. Finely chop the apricots and cut the tangerines into quarters. Mix all the ingredients together and bind with the egg.

DUCK IN HONEY SAUCE

1 duck	5 tbsp Marsala
1 oz unsalted butter	Juice of ½ lemon
1 tbsp cooking oil	Salt and black pepper
2 oz onion, chopped	½ pint single cream
2 tbsp honey	Watercress for garnish
1 sprig thyme	

Cut the duck into 4. Prick the bird well and sprinkle with salt.
Heat the oil and the butter in a large frying pan and brown the
pieces of duck. Remove and set to one side whilst you drain off the
excess fat, leaving just enough to fry the onion in. When the onion
is cooked, add the honey, thyme, Marsala and lemon juice and
return the duck to the pan. Simmer on top of the stove until the
meat is tender. Strain off the excess fat and remove the duck pieces
to a hot plate. Season the sauce and stir in the cream before
pouring over the duck.
Serve with a garnish of watercress.

STUFFED CHICKEN BREASTS

4 boneless chicken breasts	5 fl oz double cream
1 glass dry white wine	Salt and black pepper
1 cup chicken stock	1 tbsp chopped parsley
1 oz cornflour	
FOR THE STUFFING	
1 oz butter	1 oz Parmesan cheese
1 large onion, finely chopped	1 tbsp lemon juice
4 oz smoked back bacon, diced	8 oz lightly cooked broccoli spears
5 oz cream cheese	Salt and pepper

Place each chicken breast between 2 sheets of greaseproof paper
and, using a rolling pin, flatten each one a little until it covers
about twice the surface area (it should be about ¼ inch thick). Put
on one side, and proceed to make the stuffing.
Melt the butter (in a thick, small saucepan) and soften the onion,
but do not let it brown. Add the diced bacon and cook for a little
longer. Add the cream cheese and allow it to melt. Remove the
pan from the heat, and then stir in the Parmesan cheese, lemon

juice and the lightly cooked broccoli spears. Season with salt and pepper. Allow the mixture to cool and firm up a little.

Place a portion of stuffing in the centre of each chicken breast, and then fold them over and secure them with string or cocktail sticks.

Preheat the oven to gas mark 4, 350°F (180°C). Put the chicken breasts, seam-side down, in a buttered, shallow baking dish. Pour on the wine and chicken stock, and cover with foil. Bake in the oven for 45 minutes. When they are cooked, remove the chicken to a hot dish and strain off the stock into a saucepan. Blend in the cornflour and allow the sauce to thicken. Add the cream gradually and adjust the seasoning of salt and pepper, stirring until the sauce is smooth and thick. Pour over the chicken breasts and sprinkle with the chopped parsley.

LIZ BAXENDALE'S CHICKEN RICE DISH

4 chicken breasts	2 tomatoes, peeled, deseeded and
1 oz butter	chopped
Salt and black pepper	1 clove garlic, chopped
1 tbsp olive oil	½ pint chicken stock
2 onions, chopped	8-oz can pineapple juice
4 oz button mushrooms, sliced	6 oz cooked brown rice
½ green pepper, deseeded and sliced	

Preheat the oven to gas mark 5, 375°F (190°C). Dot the chicken breasts with butter and season with salt and black pepper. Cover with foil and cook in the oven for 40 minutes.

Melt the oil in a large, thick frying pan and add all the sliced vegetables. Stir fry for 2 minutes – if you have a wok, all the better, but it is not essential. Add the garlic, and then add the stock and pineapple juice. Simmer for 30 minutes, stirring continually. Finally add the cooked brown rice and cook for a further 5 minutes.

Pour the rice and vegetables into a deep serving dish and place the baked chicken joints on the top. Decorate with fresh parsley and slices of lemon.

LEMON CHICKEN

4 chicken breasts	4 oz butter

FOR THE MARINADE

4 lemons	Salt and black pepper
1 tsp thyme	1 glass dry vermouth
1 dsp chopped parsley	

Skin the chicken breasts.

Squeeze the juice from the lemons into a deep baking dish and finely grate the rind of one of them into the dish as well. Add the herbs and some salt and black pepper. Mix in the dry vermouth. Marinate the chicken breasts in the liquid for 4 hours in the refrigerator, turning once.

Preheat the oven to gas mark 4, 350°F (180°C). Lightly grease a shallow baking dish with a little of the butter, and add the chicken with the marinade. Dot with the rest of the butter and bake in the oven for 40 minutes. Serve with a green salad.

CHICKEN IN A CREAM AND BRANDY SAUCE

1 × 3 lb roasting chicken	Salt and black pepper
1 onion, peeled but whole	1 wineglass brandy
4 oz butter	5 fl oz double cream

For this dish you will need a large casserole that can be used on top of the stove.

Remove the giblets from the chicken (fresh, not frozen, if possible) and reserve them in the freezer for another occasion. Wash the chicken well and place the peeled onion inside the body cavity, along with an ounce of the butter. If you are feeling really confident, force some of the butter under the skin of the bird with your fingers, and spread a lot more over the outside of the bird. Sprinkle well with fresh ground pepper and a little salt.

Heat the remaining butter in the casserole and then proceed to place the whole chicken inside. Using a pair of forks, keep turning the bird until it is browned on every side.

Turn the heat down low and cover the casserole with some greaseproof paper and a close-fitting lid. Allow the chicken to cook slowly in the butter for about 45 minutes on top of the stove, shaking the casserole gently every few minutes just to make sure that the chicken is not sticking to the base.

Heat the brandy in a large soup ladle and at the same time turn the heat up under the chicken so that the pan is very hot as you pour the brandy on. Set fire to the brandy and then allow the flames to go down. Turn down the heat.

Have a sharp carving knife, fork and cutting board ready. Remove the chicken from the pan, joint it and cut the rest into neat portions. Keep the joints and meat warm in a covered dish and set to one side.

Allow the casserole to stand off the heat for a couple of minutes before adding the cream. Return the casserole to the heat and gently bring the sauce to the boil, allowing it to thicken before pouring it over the chicken joints in the dish.

CHICKEN BREAST PASTIES

4 chicken breasts	12 oz puff pastry
FOR THE STUFFING	
4 oz dried apricots, chopped	Rind of 1 orange
4 oz cooking apples, sliced	Salt and black pepper
1 medium onion, chopped	1 tsp dried thyme
1 oz breadcrumbs	1 beaten egg

Preheat the oven to gas mark 6, 400°F (200°C).

Place the chicken breasts between 2 sheets of greaseproof paper and beat them thin with a rolling pin or a meat hammer.

Make the stuffing by mixing the apricots, apples and onion together with the breadcrumbs and the grated rind of the orange. Season with some salt and pepper, add the dried thyme, and bind together with a little of the beaten egg.

Roll out the puff pastry and cut into 4 squares. Place a spoonful of stuffing in the centre of each chicken breast and fold over. Place each of the chicken breasts in a puff pastry square and bring the sides over to make a pasty shape. Seal down the edges with the rest of the beaten egg and glaze each pasty well with the egg.

Place the pasties on a greased baking tray and bake in the oven for 30 minutes. Serve hot or cold.

DRUMSTICKS IN CIDER

8 chicken drumsticks	2 tbsp tomato purée
8 rashers smoked bacon	¼ pint medium-sweet cider
1 oz butter	1 tsp oregano
2 medium onions, chopped	1 tsp marjoram
1 clove garlic, crushed	1 tbsp cornflour
1 × 14-oz can chopped tomatoes	Salt and black pepper

Wrap the chicken drumsticks in the bacon and place on the bottom of a casserole. Preheat the oven to gas mark 6, 400°F (200°C).

Melt the butter in a saucepan, add the chopped onion and garlic and cook until soft. Add the tomatoes, tomato purée, cider and herbs. Mix the cornflour with a little of the sauce and return to the pan. Bring to the boil and season.

Pour the sauce over the drumsticks, cover and cook in the oven for about an hour until tender.

CHICKEN BREASTS WITH APPLE SAUCE

8 chicken breasts	2 eggs
3 onions	8 oz breadcrumbs
8 cloves	1 oz butter
1 pint chicken stock	2 tbsp cooking oil
4 medium carrots	1 pint apple juice
2 bay leaves	4 dessert apples
Salt	Watercress to garnish

Skin the chicken breasts. Push the cloves into 2 of the peeled onions. Place the breasts in a casserole with the stock, the carrots, the 2 onions, bay leaves and a little salt. Cover with a firm-fitting lid and simmer for 20 minutes. Remove the chicken breasts from the stock and allow to cool.

Preheat the oven to gas mark 7, 425°F (220°C). Beat the eggs well. Roll the cooled chicken breasts in the egg, and then dip in the breadcrumbs. Melt half the butter in a frying pan and add the oil. When it is hot enough, brown the chicken joints on each side.

Slice the third onion and gently fry it in the remaining butter until it is soft but not brown. Place the fried onion on the bottom of a fairly large casserole and arrange the chicken breasts on the top. Pour on the apple juice (make sure you do not submerge the pieces of chicken altogether). Peel and cut up the apples and arrange them on top of the chicken.

Place uncovered in the centre of the oven for 20 minutes. Serve garnished with watercress.

CHICKEN PANCAKES

1½ lb cooked chicken	½ lb frozen mixed vegetables
Juice of 2 lemons	1 tbsp plain flour
Salt and black pepper	¼ tsp mustard powder
1 oz butter	¾ pint milk
½ lb button mushrooms, sliced	
FOR THE PANCAKE BATTER	
6 oz plain flour	½ pint milk
2 medium eggs	Salt and pepper

Make up the pancake mixture by blending together the eggs and flour, then gradually stirring in the milk. Season with a little salt and pepper. Place in a jug and allow to stand for a couple of hours in a refrigerator. Cut the chicken meat up into small cubes and sprinkle with the lemon juice. Allow to marinate for a couple of hours.

Melt half the butter in a thick saucepan. Add the mushrooms and cook gently before adding the mixed vegetables. Remove these from the pan and set to one side.

Add the rest of the butter to the pan and make a sauce with the flour, mustard and milk. Allow to cook for a minute, adjust the seasoning and remove from the heat. Stir in the cooked vegetables. Pour half the sauce over the chicken meat and keep the rest. Preheat the oven to gas mark 4, 350°F (180°C).

Now begin to make the pancakes. Place a spoonful of the chicken on the centre of each, fold over, and place each pancake in a buttered oven dish. There should be enough batter to make 6 to 8. Pour the remaining sauce over them and place in the oven for about 40 minutes.

COLD CHICKEN IN LEMON SAUCE

1 × 3 lb chicken	2 or 3 black peppercorns
1 small onion, peeled but whole	Salt
1 bay leaf	

FOR THE SAUCE	
½ oz butter	5 fl oz double cream
½ oz flour	Salt and black pepper
¼ pint chicken stock (see recipe)	4 oz white grapes, halved
Juice and rind of 2 lemons	Watercress
1 egg yolk	

Wash the chicken and make sure the giblets have been removed. Place the peeled onion and the bay leaf inside the chicken. Put in a pan and cover with water. Add some salt and black peppercorns, cover with a tight-fitting lid, bring to the boil, and simmer for about an hour. Let the chicken stand in the juices until it is quite cold. Remove all the meat from the bones and then place it on a serving dish. Reserve ¼ pint of the stock.

Melt the butter in a pan over a low heat and stir in the flour, cooking gently for 1 minute. Gradually stir in the stock, and bring to the boil, stirring all the time until you get a smooth sauce. Away from the heat, stir in the juice and finely grated rind of the lemons. Blend together the egg yolk and the cream, and stir into the sauce. Adjust the seasoning. Stir the grapes into the sauce, spoon it over the cold chicken and decorate with sprigs of watercress.

THE GAME LARDER

Although for centuries the squire sought to preserve his game by savage protection laws, poaching was always rife and his gamekeepers were all too often outwitted. Many of his pheasants, grouse or deer must have found their way into his tenants' stew pots. Now of course shooting rights are let out to all sorts of business interests and, with better gamekeeping, more and more birds are available on the market (though the prices at the beginning of the season still reach exorbitant levels). Look out for game dealers in your area – they will often supply game birds at very reasonable prices. And you'll find that lots of supermarkets these days sell pheasant and grouse, and even venison.

Rabbits and pigeons have always been free for the taking by whoever could trap or shoot them – in the old days they provided the only (occasional) source of protein to many an impoverished rural household. There are many traditional recipes to be sampled, and it is a mistake to think these rich meats are only to be enjoyed by the wealthy. The health-conscious should note that they are good for you, too, since they are lower in fats than other red meats. Although game is readily available in freezer cabinets, I must admit I still prefer to eat it when in season!

RABBIT CASSEROLE

1 rabbit	1 oz flour
1 oz butter	½ pint chicken stock
1 tbsp cooking oil	Salt and black pepper
1 large onion, chopped	2 oz pearl barley
4 oz bacon, cut in strips	8 oz button mushrooms

Preheat the oven to gas mark 4, 350°F (180°C). Cut the rabbit into portions. In a thick casserole melt the butter and the oil and gently brown the rabbit all over. Remove the joints and add the onions to the pan. Cook until soft. Add the bacon, then stir in the flour, stock, salt and pepper. Cook until the sauce begins to thicken.

Add the pearl barley and the rabbit joints together with the mushrooms. Cover and simmer in the centre of the oven for 1½ hours.

RABBIT PIE

1 leek, sliced	¼ level tsp mixed herbs
2 diced carrots	Salt and pepper
2 potatoes, peeled and sliced	½ pint stock
4 rabbit joints	8 oz shortcrust pastry
4 oz chopped gammon	Beaten egg
1 tbsp chopped parsley	

Preheat the oven to gas mark 7, 425°F (220°C). Fill a deep pie dish
with layers of leeks, carrots, potatoes, rabbit and gammon,
sprinkling all the way through with the parsley, herbs, salt and
pepper. Add stock to just below the rim of the pie dish. Roll out
the pastry, cover the pie dish and seal the edges well. Make a hole
in the centre. Glaze with the beaten egg.

Put the pie in the preheated oven for 5 minutes, and then turn
the oven down to gas mark 3, 325°F (170°C) for 1¼ hours.

RUTLAND HARE STEW

1 large hare, jointed	2 carrots, sliced
2 oz plain flour	6 small turnips, diced
Salt and black pepper	8 oz red cabbage, sliced
4 tbsp cooking oil	2 cloves garlic, crushed
8 oz shallots, sliced	½ pint chicken stock
1 parsnip, sliced	
FOR THE MARINADE	
1 pint red wine	1 tsp paprika
1 large onion, chopped	2 tbsp cooking oil
1 oz crushed peppercorns	

Stir all the ingredients for the marinade together briskly, then
pour over the jointed hare in a dish. Leave to marinate for 24 hours
in a cool place.

Remove the joints of the hare and roll in seasoned flour. (You
can dò this in a plastic bag.)

Heat the oil in a large casserole, then fry the shallots and
gradually add all the vegetables and garlic until they are softened
(but are not too soft). Add the stock and the marinade and bring to
the boil. Add the pieces of hare and simmer gently for 3 to 4
hours. Serve very hot.

GALANTINE OF GAME

1 rabbit or hare	1 bunch mixed herbs
1 onion, chopped	Salt
1 carrot, sliced	2 pints water
1 stick celery, sliced	4 oz tongue
1/2 lb bacon, diced	1 hard-boiled egg
1 turnip, diced	3/4 oz gelatine
10 peppercorns	

Joint the rabbit or hare and place it in a pan with the onion, carrot, celery, bacon, turnip, peppercorns and mixed herbs, a little salt and the water. Bring to the boil and simmer for about 35 minutes until the rabbit is quite tender.

Remove the rabbit and take all the meat off the bones. Return the bones to the pan and simmer them for another hour.

Neatly dice the rabbit meat and cut the tongue into strips. Arrange the sliced hard-boiled egg at the bottom of a mould and arrange the tongue and the rabbit meat on the top.

Strain the stock and dissolve the gelatine in it. When it has cooled, and almost set, pour the stock over the rabbit meat in the mould. Allow to cool and set. Chill well before serving in slices.

PIGEON CASSEROLE

1 tsp oil for frying	6 oz button mushrooms
4 oz butter	2 tbsp brandy
4 oz plain flour	1 large glass red wine
Salt and black pepper	1/2 pint chicken stock
4 dressed pigeons	Bouquet garni
1 large onion, sliced	1 bay leaf
1 clove garlic, crushed	8 juniper berries
8 rashers smoked back bacon, diced	4 oz raisins
4 oz carrot, diced	

Preheat the oven to gas mark 5, 375°F (190°C). Heat the oil and 3 ounces of butter in a thick frying pan. Season the flour and roll the pigeons in half of it. Proceed to brown the pigeons all over in the oil and butter, and place them in a casserole.

Fry the onion, garlic, bacon and carrots in the oil and butter for about 5 minutes, add the mushrooms and cook for about 2 minutes longer. Add the cooked vegetables to the pigeons in the casserole. Warm the brandy and pour it over the contents of the casserole and set it alight. Add the glass of wine before the flames die down. Pour on the stock and add the bouquet garni, bay leaf, juniper berries and the raisins. Check the seasoning, and cover with a firm-fitting lid. Cook in the oven for ½ an hour, then turn the oven down to gas mark 3, 325°F (170°C) for 1 hour more.

Soften the remaining butter and add the rest of the flour to it. Stir this into the sauce to thicken it before serving.

POACHER'S PIE

2 pigeon breasts	Pinch ground coriander
2 pheasant breasts	Rind of 1 lemon
2 pheasant legs	Salt and black pepper
4 rabbit joints	½ pint good stock
8 oz field mushrooms, sliced	8 oz wholemeal pastry
8 oz chestnuts, boiled and peeled	Beaten egg
Pinch nutmeg	

Preheat the oven to gas mark 6, 400°F (200°C).

Skin all the joints and arrange them in a large, deep pie dish along with the mushrooms, chestnuts, spices and lemon rind and sprinkle well with salt and black pepper. Cover with the stock.

Roll out the wholemeal pastry and cover the dish with it. Make a hole in the centre, seal the edges and brush with the beaten egg. Cook in the preheated oven for 20 minutes, then turn the oven down to gas mark 4, 350°F (180°C) and cook for a further hour and 10 minutes. If necessary, top up the stock through the hole in the centre.

PARTRIDGE HOT POT

2 partridges	Salt and pepper
2 oz butter	½ lb smoked bacon rashers
8 Colchester oysters	½ lb potatoes, sliced
1 onion, sliced	½ pint stock
¼ lb lamb's liver, sliced	1 glass port
1 tsp cayenne pepper	

Preheat the oven to gas mark 5, 375°F (190°C). Butter a casserole dish. Joint the partridges and place some of the pieces in the casserole. Put 4 of the oysters, some of the onion, a slice of liver and a little cayenne pepper on top, then more of the joints and another layer of oysters, onion and liver until all are used up, seasoning as you go. Cover the top with bacon and then the sliced potatoes. Pour on the stock and the port.

Cover the casserole with a close-fitting lid and bake in the oven for about 2 hours. Serve directly from the casserole.

A PIG
IN A POKE

In days gone by many a countryman kept a pig in his backyard, fattening him up on all kinds of vegetable waste, and treating him almost as a pet until the day came when he had to be slaughtered – and then nothing was wasted: what couldn't be eaten straightaway was salted or smoked, and the offal was used in sausages, faggots, black puddings . . . the list is endless. Wonderful economy, and an essential way of stretching a meagre salary to feed the large families of those days. Pigs love being left free to roam, able to root about and to take mud baths, especially on hot days. One of the best pigmen I knew as a boy in East Anglia was Alf Shingles. He loved his pigs, and they responded by winning many prizes for him in shows all over the country, including the Royal Show. Ethel, his wife, was no less devoted to them, and many was the time I've been invited into their huge kitchen to see the runt of the litter being brought back to life by her tender loving care. She'd wrap it up in an old blanket and warm it up in the coolest oven of the old-fashioned range – with the door open of course!

Because the pig puts on weight in direct proportion to what it eats, it has been subject to much intensive breeding for the commercial market. In order to reduce the risk of disease, this has meant that they have been reared in sterile conditions, in specially built concrete pig units. However, in many areas now there seems to be a reversal of that trend: and several farms around me in Worcestershire, and in other parts of the country too, are keeping their pigs in individual sties out in the fields so that the pigs can farrow and have their litters in the open. I'm quite certain that the result is happier pigs, and a contented pig puts on weight quicker.

The recipes here are as versatile as the pig itself. (There's an old saying that there's hardly a part of a pig that cannot be eaten, even down to the curl in its tail.) They combine traditional favourites with new ideas for something a bit 'different'. There's hardly an occasion when pork doesn't fit the bill, from the most festive meal, or warming winter dish, down to a quick and simple supper of bacon and potatoes.

HUNTER'S STEW

3 lb white or red cabbage	2 large cooking apples, sliced
½ lb pork ribs	2 bay leaves
½ lb ham bones	1 oz lard
½ lb garlic sausage, sliced	1 oz plain flour
½ lb smoked gammon, cubed	1 oz brown sugar
4 oz mushrooms	1 pinch cumin
1 large onion, sliced	1 pint chicken stock
1 large carrot, sliced	

For this dish you'll need a really large saucepan or casserole that can be used on the top of the stove. Shred the cabbage and place it in the pan together with the pork ribs, ham bones, garlic sausage, gammon, mushrooms, half the onion, carrots, apples and bay leaves.

In a frying pan melt the lard and fry the other half of the onion until it is golden brown, then add the flour and cook for a further minute. Add this to the pan together with the rest of the ingredients and simmer for 20 minutes, stirring regularly.

This really is an 'all-in-one dish', and is particularly good heated up the second day when all the flavours have merged.

BRAISED PORK CHOPS WITH APPLES

1 small onion, chopped	4 oz stewed apples
1 clove garlic, chopped	5 fl oz apple juice
1 small red pepper, sliced	1 tsp sage
1 small green pepper, sliced	4 pork chops (without the kidney)
1 oz butter	½ oz cornflour
1 tbsp cooking oil	

Gently fry the onions, garlic and peppers in the butter and oil until they are soft. Add the stewed apples, apple juice and sage and heat through. Finally add the pork chops and cook for 40 minutes on top of the stove in the covered pan. When the chops are cooked remove them to a serving dish and thicken the sauce with the cornflour. Serve with freshly baked potatoes.

PORK CHOPS COOKED IN ALE

4 pork chops	1 tbsp tomato purée
½ pint brown ale	1 tbsp plain flour
1 oz butter	¼ pint chicken stock
8 oz onions, sliced	Salt and pepper
1 tsp dried sage	3 large apples, peeled and sliced

Place the chops in a casserole and cover with the ale. Allow to stand for 1 hour. Preheat the oven to gas mark 4, 350°F (180°C). Melt the butter in a frying pan, add the onions and cook until they are soft. Toss in the sage and cook for a minute more. Add the contents of the pan to the chops with the tomato purée.

Blend the flour with a little of the stock and add this to the chops with the rest of the stock. Season lightly with salt and pepper and cook covered in the oven for 40 minutes. Add the apple slices (they should be fairly chunky) to the casserole 10 minutes before serving.

PORK CHOPS WITH GRAPEFRUIT

4 pork chops	¼ pint grapefruit juice
Salt and pepper	1 tsp made mustard
2 oz butter	1 tsp mixed herbs
1 medium onion, chopped	1 dsp grapefruit rind, finely grated
½ oz flour	1 whole grapefruit cut into segments
¼ pint stock	

Trim any excess fat off the pork chops and season with a little salt and pepper. Gently melt 1 ounce of the butter in a thick frying pan and gently cook the chops a little on each side. Put them in a shallow casserole dish. Add the rest of the butter to the frying pan and gently cook the onion until it is soft. Stir in the flour and allow to cook for a minute before adding the stock and the grapefruit juice. Stir continuously until the sauce thickens and then add the mustard and the herbs. Pour the sauce over the chops in the casserole. Cover with a tight-fitting lid and cook for 40 minutes very gently on top of the stove.

When cooked remove the chops onto a serving dish, sprinkle with the finely grated grapefruit rind and arrange the segments of grapefruit around the chops.

SOMERSET FILLET OF PORK

2 pork fillets, thickly sliced	Salt
6 black peppercorns	1 oz flour
1 clove garlic, crushed	1 oz butter
9 juniper berries, crushed	5 fl oz single cream
10 fl oz cider	2 eating apples, sliced
5 fl oz chicken stock	

Place the thickly sliced pork fillet in a shallow casserole with the peppercorns, garlic and juniper berries and pour on half the cider and the stock. Cover the pan and cook in a moderate oven for 1 hour. Remove the pork fillet slices to a serving dish and add the rest of the cider and the stock to the pan. Rapidly boil for a few minutes until the sauce has reduced by one-third, and adjust the seasoning.

Blend the flour and butter together and stir into the sauce. Cook until it thickens. Add the cream and pour over the fillets. Serve decorated with slices of apple.

PORK AND PINEAPPLE CASSEROLE

2 lb lean pork, cubed	¼ pint chicken stock
2 oz butter	¾ pint milk
1 tbsp oil	1 bay leaf
1 large onion, chopped	Salt and pepper
3 sticks celery, sliced	4 oz sweetcorn
3 carrots, sliced	1 small tin pineapple chunks
1 oz cornflour	5 fl oz single cream

Brown the pork cubes gently in the butter and oil melted in a 3-pint casserole. Remove, and add the onion, celery and carrot and cook, stirring all the time, for a few minutes. Return the pork to the casserole and stir in the cornflour, stock and milk and add the bay leaf and seasoning. Simmer well on top of the stove for 45 minutes, being sure to stir the casserole from time to time.

After the 45 minutes cooking time add the sweetcorn and the drained pineapple chunks. (If you think the sauce is too thick add a little of the pineapple juice.) Cook for a further 15 minutes and just before serving stir in the cream.

GAMMON IN CIDER

3 lb piece of gammon	1 tbsp butter
2 bay leaves	1 tbsp flour
6 peppercorns	5 fl oz apple juice
2 onions, sliced	A pinch pepper
1 pint dry cider	

Place the gammon joint in a large pan and cover with water. Allow to soak overnight and in the morning throw away the water. Add the bay leaves, peppercorns and onions to the pan with the gammon. Pour in enough cider to cover. Bring to the boil and simmer for about 1 hour. Remove the piece of gammon to a serving dish.

Melt the butter in a small saucepan and add the flour. Cook for 1 minute, then gradually add the apple juice. Season with pepper as necessary (no salt). Stir this sauce into the cider liquor, and serve with the hot gammon. Swedes or turnips go very well with this dish.

BREAKFAST SAUSAGE PLAIT

12 oz puff pastry	1 oz butter
1 lb prime quality sausagemeat	4 eggs
1 onion, chopped	1 tbsp milk
1 tsp mixed herbs	Salt and black pepper
6 rashers green back bacon	1 beaten egg

Preheat the oven to gas mark 4, 350°F (180°C). Roll the puff pastry out into a rectangle 14″ × 10″. Mix the sausagemeat with the onion and mixed herbs. Derind the bacon, and lay the rashers across the width of the puff pastry from long side to long side. Roll the sausagemeat into a long sausage about 12 inches long and place it longways down the middle of the bacon rashers.

Melt the butter in a thick saucepan, beat the eggs into it, adding a little milk and seasoning, and stir until they are scrambled. Make a large cut in the sausagemeat lengthways and fill the cavity with the scrambled egg. Fold the ends of the bacon rashers over the sausagemeat and eggs.

Brush the pastry with the beaten egg and then make 9 incisions down each side of pastry at 45 degrees to the sausagemeat, a little like a sergeant's stripes. Fold in each end of the pastry over the sausagemeat so that you seal it at top and bottom, and then criss-cross the pastry strips over the roll so that you end up with a plaited effect. Brush well with egg and then bake in the preheated oven for 40 minutes.

This can be served hot or cold, and makes an ideal alternative breakfast treat – I particularly like to prepare one when we are setting off on holiday in the early hours of the morning, and cut into it as we go across the Channel on the ferry!

PORK SAVOURIES

1 lb pig's liver	*½ level tsp dried sage*
8 oz onions, finely chopped	*Salt and black pepper*
2 oz suet	*A little plain flour*
10 oz breadcrumbs	

Preheat the oven to gas mark 4, 350°F (180°C). Mince the liver and mix it with the onions, suet, breadcrumbs, sage and a little salt and pepper. Dust your hands with flour and roll the mixture into about 9 balls. Put them into a baking tray or shallow oven dish so that they are closely fitting, and cover lightly with greased foil and bake at the top of the oven for 1 hour. They are delicious served with an onion gravy.

POOR MAN'S BACON FEAST

1 oz butter	*1 lb streaky bacon rashers*
½ lb onions, sliced	*Salt and white pepper*
1 lb potatoes, sliced	

Preheat the oven to gas mark 5, 375°F (190°C).

Butter the sides of a 3-inch deep oven dish. Place in it alternate layers of onion, potato and bacon, seasoning as you go with salt and pepper, making sure that you end up with the bacon on the top. Bake the dish in the middle of the oven for about 1 hour.

My mother always used to make this dish towards the end of the week. It is one of the most delicious suppertime treats I remember as a boy.

STUFFED BAKED MARROW

1 medium-sized marrow	1 lb premium sausagemeat
1 oz butter	4 oz breadcrumbs
1 onion, finely chopped	Salt and pepper
2 tomatoes, peeled and chopped	1 tsp dried sage
4 oz smoked back bacon, diced	

Preheat the oven to gas mark 4, 350°F (180°C). Slice the marrow in half lengthways and remove and discard the seeds. Melt the butter in a frying pan and gently cook the onion, tomato and bacon. Add the sausagemeat and cook until brown, then stir in the breadcrumbs, seasoning and herbs. Stuff this mixture into one half of the marrow. Put the other half of the marrow on top and wrap in greased foil. Place on a baking sheet and cook in the oven for 1¼ hours.

Serve in slices with a hot tomato sauce.

LIVER STROGANOFF

1 lb thinly sliced pig's liver	1 tbsp olive oil
2 tbsp plain flour	8 oz onions, sliced
Salt and pepper	1 can whole tomatoes
A pinch dried thyme	1 tsp dried sage
3 oz butter	5 fl oz soured cream

Toss the liver in the flour which has been seasoned with the salt, pepper and thyme, and place to one side. In a thick frying pan melt the butter and olive oil and gently fry the onion. Add the tomatoes and heat them through. Push to one side of the pan, and add the liver. Cook quickly for about 5 minutes. Sprinkle the sage over, and mix the liver with the onion and tomatoes. Reduce the heat and add the soured cream, making sure you combine all the ingredients again, and if necessary add some more salt and pepper.

Serve with freshly cooked green noodles.

LAMB'S
TALES

I've known three shepherds in my life: Cecil Fawkes, who lived and worked with a fine flock of Suffolk sheep on a large estate in Norfolk; Charlie Peck, who is my Godfather; and my father himself. All would agree that you need a fat lamb to make good meat. Cecil was a real character who lived the rural life to the full. He always enjoyed a glass or two, or rather a cup or two, to keep the winter cold out, and he knew his sheep well. My father learnt a lot from him. When Charlie Peck and his wife moved away from Suffolk all the way across the border to Essex, my father took over his flock. It is thirty years since my father retired as a shepherd, and I wonder what he and his colleagues would make of the lean carcases displayed recently at the Royal Show. Hardly any fat to be seen; they say it is what the customer wants, but I fear that only shows how little taste we must have today. Quite recently my butcher proudly displayed some lamb he had grown himself on his farm which had hardly a millimetre of fat on it. He persuaded me to try some, so I did and was not convinced, so I tried again – and still am not convinced. It may just be prejudice, but I'm sure the flavour was better in former days!

Something that seems to have disappeared from our lives is a good old-fashioned stew. They've all given way to casseroles. But there's nothing like a good neck of mutton stew to revive the weather-weary in the coldest of winters, and it is an excellent dish to serve up a second time – reheating only improves its flavour. It's also a cheap and economical dish. Though it's almost impossible to obtain mutton these days, best end of lamb makes a flavoursome substitute. In fact, you'll find plenty of ideas here, old and new, from all over the country to make the most of lamb.

THE PRINCE'S ROAST LEG OF LAMB

1 leg of lamb (not too lean)	Salt and black pepper
4 cloves of garlic, thinly sliced	2 lb potatoes, peeled and sliced

This is a French method of roasting a leg of lamb (which was in fact given to me by a Polish prince, now a wine grower in the Loire valley, who spoke perfect aristocratic English!). It seems to me to bring out all the flavour of the meat just as we used to enjoy it in England in the old days.

Using a sharp, pointed knife, make deep but small incisions in the flesh of the lamb, and then push in slivers of the garlic. Rub the lamb with salt and black pepper.

Wash, peel and slice the potatoes, and dry them well. (Parboil them if you like your potatoes really soft and floury.) Place the potatoes in a fairly deep oven dish and put it in the oven. Put the leg of lamb on the rack above so that all the juices fall on the potatoes as it cooks.

The cooking time depends on how you like your lamb. The French tend to eat their lamb terribly pink, but I myself dislike it that way. I suggest that you cook the joint at gas mark 5, 375°F (190°C) for 25 minutes per pound.

COLONIAL GOOSE

1 leg of lamb	1 small clove garlic, finely chopped
4 oz breadcrumbs	1 tsp dried thyme, or use fresh sprigs
4 oz chopped dried apricots	Salt and black pepper
1 oz butter	1 beaten egg
2 tbsp clear honey	1 sprig rosemary
2 oz grated onion	

Ask your butcher to bone the leg of lamb for you. Keep the bone to use for stock.

Mix together the breadcrumbs and chopped apricots. Melt the butter in a saucepan and add the honey. Stir together well. Grate in the onion and add the finely chopped garlic. Stir in the breadcrumb and apricot mixture with the thyme, and season with salt and black pepper. Remove from the heat and add the beaten egg.

Lay the sprig of rosemary in the bone cavity of the leg of lamb and add the stuffing. Roll up and secure with string. Weigh the stuffed joint and cook as per a leg of lamb in a moderate oven at gas mark 4, 350°F (180°C) for 2 to 2½ hours, depending upon the weight of the joint, allowing 25 minutes per pound.

Where this dish got its name from I have no idea!

ROAST BREAST OF LAMB WITH VEGETABLES

1 boned breast of lamb	2 large carrots
Salt and black pepper	4 sticks celery, washed and trimmed
1 large onion, finely chopped	2 sprigs of rosemary
1 clove garlic, finely chopped	

Preheat the oven to gas mark 5, 375°F (190°C).

Lay open the breast of lamb and rub with some salt and black pepper. Mix the chopped onion and garlic together and spread over the lamb. Cut the carrots into 4 lengthways, so that you have 8 long pieces. Lay these pieces at even distances along the open breast along with the sticks of celery and sprigs of rosemary. Carefully roll the breast of lamb up, enclosing the vegetables, and tie firmly with some string.

Bake in the oven on a trivet to drain off all the juices, allowing 25 minutes per pound.

Pour the fat from the juices, and make into gravy by adding some of the cooking water from any accompanying vegetables, possibly a glass of dry sherry, and some thickening.

SUFFOLK LAMB CUTLETS

4 lamb cutlets	12 oz puff pastry
Salt and pepper	1 well-beaten egg
FOR THE STUFFING	
1 oz butter	4 oz sultanas
1 shallot, finely chopped	4 oz smoked bacon, chopped
6 oz dried apricots, cooked and puréed	Salt and black pepper

Sprinkle the cutlets with salt and pepper and grill them. Leave them to one side.

Make the stuffing. Melt the butter and gently cook the chopped shallot until soft. Stir in the puréed apricots and the sultanas, and cook for 3 minutes more. Sweat the chopped bacon in a dry frying pan, then mix with the apricot mixture. Season and allow to cool.

Preheat the oven to gas mark 7, 425°F (220°C).

Roll the pastry out and divide it into 4 squares large enough to envelop each of the chops. Put a spoonful of the stuffing in the centre of the pastry and place a chop on top. Cover with some more stuffing. Dampen the pastry edges with the beaten egg. Bring the sides together and seal the edges of the envelopes well. Place on a baking tray and bake in the oven for 15 minutes.

SHERRIED KIDNEYS

12 lamb's kidneys	¼ pint stock
1 large onion, finely chopped	1 wineglass sherry
2 oz unsalted butter	1 clove garlic, chopped
1 tsp ground rosemary	Salt and pepper
1 oz flour	2 tbsp soured cream

Core and cut the kidneys in half lengthways. Melt 1 ounce of butter in a thick frying pan and cook the onion until it is soft, but not browned. Add the kidneys and cook a little on each side. Remove from the pan and keep hot.

Add the rest of the butter and the rosemary to the pan and blend in the flour, stirring until all the fat is soaked up. Gradually add the stock and the sherry with the clove of garlic. Season with salt and pepper. Add the kidneys, and simmer gently for 5 minutes until cooked and the sauce has thickened. Just before serving, pour on the soured cream.

SKEWERS OF LAMB

4 lamb's kidneys	8 bay leaves
1 lb lean lamb, cubed	8 button mushrooms
FOR THE MARINADE	
3 tbsp olive oil	1 small onion, chopped
3 tbsp cider vinegar	½ tsp ground ginger
1 tbsp clear honey	½ tsp cumin

The first thing to do is to make the marinade. In a thick saucepan gently heat together the olive oil, vinegar, honey, chopped onion, ground ginger and cumin. Allow to boil, and then cool.

Peel and core the kidneys before slicing in half. Place with the cubed meat in a shallow dish and pour over the marinade. Cover and leave for 4 hours in a cool place.

Arrange the meat, kidneys, bay leaves and mushrooms alternately on 4 long skewers. Grill or barbecue them slowly until they are cooked, basting with the marinade.

BEST END NECK OF MUTTON STEW

1½ lb best end neck of mutton	Salt and white pepper
1 large onion, sliced	1 heaped tsp mixed herbs
½ lb carrots, sliced	1 lb potatoes, sliced
4 sticks celery, sliced	1 pint chicken stock
1 lb swede, diced	

The smell of this delicious stew cooking takes me straight back to my childhood, with the east wind in winter blowing across the fields of East Anglia as we struggled home from the village school through the snow. As we opened the cottage door we were greeted by a truly wonderful aroma . . .

Ask your butcher to chop up the best end of neck for you into a lot of mini chops.

Slice the onion and place it at the bottom of a large casserole. Add a layer of sliced carrots and then a layer of lamb chops, a layer of celery, another layer of lamb, and then a layer of diced swede, seasoning as you go with the salt, white pepper and herbs. Top it all off with a layer of sliced potatoes, and then pour just enough stock over to cover all the ingredients except the potatoes. (If you wish you can add a little gravy browning or a little caramel to darken the stock.) Butter one side of a piece of greaseproof paper and place it over the potatoes and put the casserole lid on top.

Place the casserole on top of the stove and let it simmer very slowly for about an hour and a half. Or, if you prefer, put it in a very slow oven for a few hours.

LEICESTER LAMB CRUMBLE

1 lb cold roast lamb	½ level tsp mixed herbs
2 onions	Salt and pepper
5 oz plain flour	2 oz butter
1 tbsp tomato purée	2 oz Red Leicester cheese, grated
½ pint stock	

Cut the cold lamb up into chunks and place in a food processor along with the onion. Mince coarsely. Spread the meat and onion mixture on the bottom of an oval pie dish about 3 inches deep, and sprinkle with a little flour (about ½ an ounce). Blend the tomato purée and the stock, and pour over the mince. Sprinkle over the mixed herbs and a little salt and pepper.

Rub the rest of the flour and the butter to a crumbly texture, and then stir in the grated cheese. Spoon the crumble mixture over the mince, and bake in the oven for about 50 minutes at gas mark 5, 375°F (190°C).

LAMB AND PARSNIP PIE

2 lb parsnips	5 fl oz gravy
2 oz butter	Salt
1 tsp made mustard	2 oz cheddar cheese, grated
2 tbsp milk	2 tbsp white breadcrumbs
8 oz cooked minced lamb	

Peel and slice the parsnips, removing the woody centres. Boil in some slightly salted water until soft. Drain, and add 1 ounce of the butter, the mustard and milk, and mash together well.

Stir the gravy into the lamb and add a little salt. Butter a shallow oven dish and spread half the parsnip mixture over the bottom of the dish. Sprinkle with one half of the cheese. Spread the meat on top, and the remaining parsnip mixture on top of that. Sprinkle with the breadcrumbs and the remaining cheese. Dot with the rest of the butter and bake in the oven at gas mark 4, 350°F (180°C) for 20 to 30 minutes.

BEEFING
IT UP

What could be more traditional than beef? The roast beef of
Olde England, succulent and tender with its marbling of fat,
surrounded by crisp roast potatoes, a light and airy Yorkshire
pudding, fragrant gravy – and accompanied of course by a fiery
horseradish sauce: it conjures up images of Dickensian feasts, of
groaning boards, gleaming silver, polished mahogany . . .

Today, though, beef has fallen into some disfavour, not only
because health pundits tend to frown on its high fat content, but
because some of the cuts – the fillet and rump, or porterhouse and
entrecôte steaks, for example – are outrageously expensive. Yet
most of us have all number of ways of contriving cheap and filling
meals from minced beef, be it bolognese sauce or chilli con carne
or meat loaf, and I think it's a sad mistake if we ignore some of the
other cheaper cuts as well. With slow and steady cooking, these
can be the basis for some really delicious and satisfying meals, and
this is where it's helpful to turn to some of the traditional ways of
cooking beef. We all take the partnership of steak and kidney for
granted, forgetting that the kidney was added in the first place to
help it go a little bit further – and of course to enrich and flavour
the gravy. Don't ignore it – with a meltingly crisp pastry crust, a
good, old-fashioned steak and kidney pie can bring a lordly touch
to any meal.

We all have grim memories of greasy, bullet-like dumplings
from our school-days, but if you take care to mix in the suet with
your fingertips and add the dumplings to your stew or casserole
towards the end of the cooking time, when the gravy is really
bubbling, they will rise to the top and be as light and fluffy as
anything. They, too, were a way of padding out the meat when,
with many mouths to feed from one pot, the younger children
would be given half a dumpling, a carrot or a turnip and some
gravy, while Dad scoffed the rest! The same goes for the suet crust
on a traditional beef pudding – this does not need to be heavy if the
dough is made carefully, and I believe there is no better energy
food around when concentrated muscle work is in the offing, be it
digging the garden or playing football for England!

BEEF WITH HORSERADISH SAUCE

1 large onion, sliced	½ tsp salt
2 oz butter	Black pepper
2 lb stewing steak, cubed	¾ pint water
1 tsp curry powder	½ pint (10 fl oz) soured cream
½ tsp ground ginger	1 tbsp strong horseradish sauce
1 tsp demerara sugar	Chopped parsley
1 tbsp Worcestershire sauce	

Soften the onion in the butter in a casserole. Toss in the stewing steak and add the curry powder, ground ginger, demerara sugar, Worcestershire sauce, salt, pepper and water. Cover the casserole with a tight-fitting lid and cook in a low oven at gas mark 2, 300°F (150°C) for 2½ to 3 hours, until the meat is really tender.

Blend the soured cream with the horseradish sauce. Remove the meat onto a hot serving dish, then stir the soured cream and horseradish into the gravy. Pour over the meat, decorate with the parsley, and serve immediately.

BEEF PUDDING

1 lb stewing beef, cubed	1 oz lard
4 oz ox kidney, cored and cut up	½ lb onions, sliced
1 oz plain flour seasoned with salt and black pepper	1 bay leaf
	¼ pint beef stock
FOR THE SUET PASTRY	
12 oz self-raising flour	Salt
6 oz shredded suet	A little water

Toss the meat in the seasoned flour. Melt the lard in a thick frying pan and brown the meat all over. Remove and set to one side. Cook the onions gently in the fat until soft and add them to the meat.

Mix together the flour, suet, salt and a little water to make a light dough. Roll out two-thirds of it to line a 2-pint basin, and fill it with the meat and onions. Add the bay leaf and pour in the stock. Damp the edges of the dough, use the remaining pastry to make a lid and seal it on top of the pudding. Tie a muslin cover firmly over the basin, or use a layer of greaseproof paper and foil. Place the basin in a pan half-filled with cold water, bring gradually to the boil and simmer for about 3½ hours, checking regularly that the pan does not boil dry.

At the end of the cooking time, loosen round the edges with a knife. Turn out onto a warmed serving dish and serve with boiled potatoes and buttered carrots.

BEEF AND CARROT CASSEROLE WITH DUMPLINGS

2 lb braising steak, cut thick	4 sticks celery, sliced
2 tbsp seasoned plain flour	¾ pint beef stock
1 lb carrots, sliced	2 bay leaves
1 lb onions, sliced	
FOR THE DUMPLINGS	
4 oz self-raising flour	Salt and white pepper
2 oz suet	Water

Preheat the oven to gas mark 6, 400°F (200°C). Dip each slice of braising steak in the seasoned flour and coat well. Arrange layers of the meat and sliced vegetables in a 3-pint casserole, sprinkle any remaining flour over, and pour on the hot stock. (Add a little gravy browning or caramel if you like a dark gravy.) Push the bay leaves in, cover with greaseproof paper and a lid, and cook in the centre of the oven for 2 hours.

Meanwhile, make the dumplings. Sift the self-raising flour into a cold bowl and add the suet together with a pinch of salt and a little white pepper. Mix together with a fork and begin to add a little water, using your fingertips. When you have a suitable dough, lightly roll the mixture into 4 or 6 balls. Add the dumplings to the casserole 30 minutes before the cooking time ends and cook uncovered.

SALT BEEF WITH DUMPLINGS

3 lb joint of salt beef	2 sticks celery, sliced
10 whole shallots	8 oz parsnips, quartered
1 peeled onion, stuck with 4 cloves	Bouquet garni
8 oz small carrots, sliced	6 black peppercorns

FOR THE DUMPLINGS

4 oz self-raising flour	A pinch of mixed herbs
2 oz shredded suet	Water to mix
A pinch of salt	

Place the whole piece of beef in a large saucepan or casserole and cover with water. Bring to the boil and simmer for 5 minutes before draining the water off.

Add all the vegetables to the casserole along with the bouquet garni and peppercorns, and cover with water. Place on the lid and put to simmer on top of the stove for 2 hours.

Mix together the flour, suet, salt and herbs for the dumplings, and add a little water. Make into a firm dough and divide into 8 little balls. Add them to the cooking pot for 15 minutes at the end of the cooking time. Place the joint on a serving dish, and surround with the vegetables and dumplings.

STEAK AND KIDNEY PIE

1 lb braising steak	A pinch nutmeg
¼ lb lamb's kidney	A little gravy browning
2 oz plain flour	1 bay leaf
Salt and black pepper	¼ pint beef stock
¼ tsp thyme	8 oz puff pastry
½ lb onions, sliced	1 beaten egg
6 oz button mushrooms	

Preheat the oven to gas mark 5, 375°F (190°C). Cut the meat into strips about 3 inches long and half an inch wide. Core and cut up the kidneys. Season the flour with the salt, black pepper and thyme, and toss the meat in it. Place in a 1½-pint pie dish with the onions and the mushrooms (left whole if small, otherwise halved) and sprinkle over any remaining flour, the nutmeg and a little gravy browning. Add the bay leaf and pour the beef stock over.

Roll out the puff pastry to make a lid, and make a double edge to seal it on. Make a hole in the centre, and brush with beaten egg. Cook in the preheated oven for 20 minutes, then reduce the heat to gas mark 4, 350°F (180°C) for a further hour.

STUFFED VEAL ESCALOPES WITH TOMATO SAUCE

4 veal escalopes	Black pepper
6 oz sausagemeat	1 large egg, beaten
4–6 oz gammon, minced	2 oz plain flour
1 clove garlic, crushed	2 oz butter
6 coriander seeds, crushed	1 tbsp cooking oil
FOR THE TOMATO SAUCE	
2 tbsp oil	1 lb tomatoes, peeled and chopped
1 large onion, chopped	½ tsp oregano
Salt and black pepper	

Place each escalope between 2 sheets of greaseproof paper and beat out well with a rolling pin.

Mix together the sausagemeat, coarsely minced gammon, garlic and coriander seeds, and season with the black pepper but no salt at this stage. Divide the mixture into 4 balls. Place one in the centre of each escalope and fold round the edges. Secure with string.

Dip each stuffed escalope in the beaten egg and roll in the plain flour. Melt the butter and oil together in a thick frying pan and gently cook the escalopes through, turning all the time until they are brown on the outside. Set aside and keep warm.

Heat the oil for the tomato sauce in a thick saucepan, add the onion and cook until soft. Season with salt and black pepper, add the tomatoes and the oregano and cook until it has reduced to a good thick consistency. Pour the sauce into a heated serving dish and arrange the escalopes in it.

BEEF CASSEROLE WITH ORANGES

2 tbsp cooking oil	½ pint beef stock
1½ lb braising steak, cut in chunks	2 large oranges
8 oz onions, sliced	1 tbsp black treacle
1 clove garlic, crushed	3 tbsp brandy
2 tbsp plain flour	4 oz button mushrooms
1 tbsp tomato purée	Salt and black pepper

Heat the oil in a frying pan and seal the meat on every side. Remove to a casserole, and then fry the onions and garlic in the same fat until they are soft. Lift out with a slotted spoon and transfer to the casserole. Stir the flour into the fat and cook for 1 minute. Add the tomato purée, then gradually pour in the stock, stirring all the time, and bring to the boil. Finely pare the rind of the oranges into the sauce, and add the juice as well, with the treacle and the brandy. Add the mushrooms (quartered if large ones) and season with salt and pepper. Pour the sauce over the meat in the casserole. Cover with a firm-fitting lid and cook for 2 hours at gas mark 3, 325°F (170°C).

Check the seasoning before serving and boil to reduce the stock if necessary. Serve with some plain boiled potatoes.

BEEF AND PEPPER CASSEROLE

2 lb chuck steak, cut in strips	1 clove garlic, crushed
2 level tbsp flour	1 red pepper, deseeded and sliced
Salt and black pepper	1 green pepper, deseeded and sliced
1 level tsp paprika	1 pint stock
2 tbsp cooking oil	1 tbsp tomato purée
1 large onion, sliced	5 fl oz yoghurt

Preheat the oven to gas mark 4, 350°F (180°C). Toss the meat in the flour which has been seasoned with salt, pepper and paprika. Heat the oil in a large frying pan and gently fry the onions, garlic and peppers. Transfer them to a deep casserole dish. Brown the meat in the oil and add to the casserole. Pour in the stock and the tomato purée and cook in the centre of the oven for 1 hour.

Just before serving, spoon over the yoghurt.

JELLIED BEEF IN CIDER

2 lb topside beef	2 oz lard
2 pig's trotters	Bunch of mixed herbs
2 lb onions, sliced	Salt and black pepper
2 lb carrots, sliced	1 pint strong cider
Larding fat	1 wineglass port

Ask your butcher to wrap the beef up in the larding fat and tie well. (Alternatively, you can do it yourself by pushing strips of bacon fat into the beef using a special needle – it will end up looking like a hedgehog!) Ask him to split the pig's trotters too.

Melt the lard in a large casserole and gently fry the onions. Place the beef on top of the onions with the pig's trotters and pack well all round with the carrots. Add the mixed herbs and season with salt and pepper. Pour on enough cider to cover the joint.

Cover the casserole with a tight-fitting lid and simmer very gently on top of the stove 2 to 3 hours. Carefully strain off the juices and allow the beef and the juices to cool thoroughly. The juices will jellify.

Slice the beef and arrange on a serving dish. Remove the fat from the top of the jellified stock and gently heat the stock through. Add the port and stir well. Strain once more and allow to set a little before spooning over the beef. Chill until the stock has set completely. Or you can allow the jelly to set separately, then chop it up and decorate the beef with it.

This makes a really superb central dish for a summer buffet. It's best made a few days beforehand, and kept chilled. Serve it with lots of salads. It really is delicious, and looks quite stunning.

MINCED BEEF COBBLER

1 large onion, chopped	1 can tomatoes, chopped
2 tbsp oil	¼ pint water
1½ lb best minced beef	1 tsp mixed herbs
2 beef stock cubes	Salt and black pepper

FOR THE TOPPING

8 oz self-raising flour	A pinch of salt
4 oz suet	A little water

Preheat the oven to gas mark 6, 400°F (200°C). Chop the onion and fry gently in the oil until it is soft. Add the minced beef and brown well. Sprinkle over the stock cubes and add the chopped tomatoes, water, mixed herbs and seasoning.

Cover and cook for about 30 minutes in the oven.

Mix together the flour, suet and salt with a little water and roll out to make scone shapes. (You can add a little sage to the flour if you wish.) They need only be roughly made, so shape them by hand.

When the meat is ready, remove from the oven and take off the lid. Place the scones carefully on top of the mince and cook for a further 20 minutes in the oven until the scones are golden brown.

PUDDINGS GALORE

Never let it be said that the British lack imagination when it comes to the art of pudding making. Some of the best recipes we have stretch right back to the eighteenth century and beyond, though the fashion for confining the sweet dish to the end of the meal is comparatively recent. In medieval times the only sweeteners came from fruits or honey, and it was then very usual to mix meat and savoury things with raisins or oranges or plums to make rich, highly spiced dishes (ginger was a highly prized flavouring). This is the origin of the mincemeat we all eat so happily at Christmas in our piping hot mince pies – once there would have been as much meat as fruit in the mixture.

Anyway, whether it be cold puddings – syllabubs, fools and flummeries, making the most of our fruits in due season – or hot puddings – steamed or baked, flans, tarts or charlottes – we really do excel at them. You only have to watch the elderly gentleman consuming his bread and butter pudding in the dining room of his club to realise how important puddings are to us, and how much they remind us of our childhoods. It may be that children today do not have quite the sweet tooth they used to – certainly dentists have been waging a campaign to cut down the amount of white sugar we all use, and quite rightly too, since there is no doubt our teeth will be all the better for doing without it. But so far as I'm concerned, there'll always be room for a well-chosen pudding to round off the perfect meal – and if a lot of my favourites here seem to rely on a goodly amount of cream and a dash of liqueur, well I'm afraid my besetting sin is not unknown to you. . . .

GOLDEN COLDIES

MINTED GRAPEFRUIT SORBET

7 fl oz water	1 tbsp grated grapefruit rind
3 oz sugar	½ pint grapefruit juice
1 sprig fresh mint	1 egg white

Dissolve the sugar in the water and bring to the boil. Add the mint and simmer for 5 minutes. Stand to one side and allow to cool. Remove the mint then stir in the grapefruit rind and the juice. Pour the mixture into a freezer tray and freeze until granular.

Beat the egg white until it is frothy and fold into the ice mixture. Replace in the freezer tray and freeze again until it is firm. Serve in chilled glasses with some grated rind on top.

LEMON DELIGHT

½ pint lemon jelly made with 1 pkt	5 fl oz cream cheese
5 fl oz double cream	1 oz dark chocolate, grated

Make up the half pint of lemon jelly. In a food processor or mixer whisk together the cream and the cream cheese, and finally blend in the cooled lemon jelly (it should be nearly set). Pour into glasses and chill well in the refrigerator.

Decorate with the grated chocolate just before serving.

CRANACHAN

1 tbsp clear heather honey	8 oz fresh raspberries
3 tbsp whisky liqueur	2 oz fine toasted oatmeal
10 fl oz double cream	

Blend the honey and whisky liqueur together by heating them gently in a pan and then allow them to cool. Whip the cream until it is thick and blend with the honey and whisky.

Put alternate layers of the cream, raspberries and oatmeal in individual tall glasses, ending up with a layer of cream. Decorate with a few raspberries.

COFFEE MOUSSE

1 sachet gelatine	2 oz castor sugar
1/4 cup water	1/2 cup strong black coffee (see recipe)
3 eggs, separated	10 fl oz double cream

Sprinkle the sachet of gelatine onto the water in a cup and allow to stand until it has set. Place the cup in a saucepan of water and heat gently. When it has melted, allow to cool a little.

Meanwhile, beat the egg yolks with the sugar until they reach a good creamy consistency. Make some really strong coffee by adding 2 heaped teaspoonfuls of coffee powder to a 1/2-cupful of boiling water (if you are using real coffee, make it twice the usual strength). Whisk the coffee into the egg yolks and sugar mixture. By this time the melted gelatine should have cooled enough to beat into the mixture. Allow this to stand until it begins to thicken.

Now whisk the egg whites until they peak well, and fold in. Whip the cream until thick and fold that in too: do not be too violent doing this (it's not advisable to make this dish if you've had a tiff with the one you love!).

Tie a collar of greaseproof paper around a 7-inch soufflé dish and spoon in the mixture. Cover with film and chill in the fridge. Decorate the top with some piped cream or coffee vermicelli before serving.

CHOCOLATE WHIP

10 oz double cream	1 tsp instant coffee powder
2 oz castor sugar	1 sachet gelatine
6 tbsp water	1 tbsp rum
2 tsp drinking chocolate powder	2 oz grated plain chocolate

Whip together the cream and the castor sugar until thick. In a small saucepan heat together the water, chocolate powder, coffee powder and gelatine until all is dissolved and well blended. Remove from the heat and allow to cool for a minute before stirring in the rum.

Beat this mixture into the cream, but not too fiercely, else it may well turn runny. Spoon the mixture into some sundae glasses and grate a little plain chocolate onto each. Serve with sponge fingers or langue de chat biscuits.

STRAWBERRIES . . .
as they are in Heaven!

1 lb hulled strawberries	2 tbsp Grand Marnier
4 level tbsp vanilla sugar	1 tsp finely grated orange rind
2 tbsp crème de cacao	1 tbsp desiccated coconut

Cut the strawberries into quarters and then sprinkle them with the vanilla sugar (that is, castor sugar in which you have stored a vanilla pod for some considerable time). Sprinkle the strawberries with the liqueurs and the orange rind and cover the bowl with cling film before placing in the fridge to chill well.

Just before serving sprinkle with the desiccated coconut.

DEVIL'S DELIGHT

2 nectarines	10 fl oz double cream
6 tbsp brandy	2 oz light muscavado sugar
12 oz fresh raspberries	

Cut up the nectarines and divide them between 4 to 6 individual glasses. Pour a tablespoonful of brandy over each. Put the raspberries, double cream and sugar in a food processor until it is all blended and has begun to thicken a little. Spoon some of the sauce onto each of the glasses and place in the fridge to chill.

Place one raspberry in the centre of each glass and sprinkle a little demerara sugar over just before serving.

PEACH AND ORANGE
INSTANT DESSERT

½ pint double cream	1 large orange, peeled and sliced
½ pint soured cream	3 oz toasted nuts, chopped
1 large peach, peeled and sliced	1 tbsp demerara sugar

Whisk the double cream until it is fairly stiff and then whip in the soured cream. Fold the fruit into the cream and spoon into glasses. Sprinkle with the chopped nuts and demerara sugar. Chill and serve.

APPLE SNOW

1½ lb cooking apples	A pinch of cinnamon
1 oz butter	Juice and rind of ½ lemon
4 oz castor sugar	2 egg whites

Peel and slice the apples and place them in a thick saucepan with the knob of butter, add 2 ounces of the sugar and a drop of water. Place the lid on the pan and cook gently until they have collapsed and lost their shape. Stir in the rest of the sugar, the cinnamon, and the juice and finely grated rind of the lemon. Allow to cool.

Whisk the egg whites until they are really stiff and then fold into the apple purée mixture. Chill, and serve soon after making.

GOOSEBERRY FOOL

2 lb gooseberries	1 egg yolk
3 oz sugar	½ pint milk
2 tbsp water	5 fl oz double cream

Wash the gooseberries and place them in a thick saucepan with 2 ounces of the sugar and water. Cook slowly covered with a close-fitting lid. Purée the cooked gooseberries in a food processor.

Beat the egg yolk and the remaining 1 ounce of sugar together. Bring the milk to the boil and pour onto the egg mixture. Return to the pan and cook very gently until the custard thickens, and then allow to cool.

Mix the purée and the custard together. Whip the double cream and fold in carefully. Pour into individual glasses and chill.

RHUBARB CHARLOTTE

1½ lb rhubarb	2 oz gingernut biscuits, crushed
Juice and grated rind of 1 orange	4 oz chopped walnuts
4 oz demerara sugar	½ tsp cinnamon
2 oz butter	Whipped double cream to decorate

Wash and clean the rhubarb, and cut it into 2-inch slices. Cover the bottom of a thick pan with water and add the rhubarb with the juice and finely grated rind of the orange. Add half the sugar and gently simmer the rhubarb until it is just cooked, but has not lost its shape.

Melt the butter in a thick saucepan and add the crushed biscuits, chopped nuts and cinnamon. Cook gently for 3 minutes.

Drain the juice from the rhubarb. Reserve a few pieces. Spoon alternate layers of rhubarb and the biscuit mixture into a glass bowl, ending up with a layer of biscuit. Decorate the top with twirls of cream and the reserved pieces of rhubarb, and sprinkle the remaining sugar over. Chill and serve.

JUBILEE PUDDING

1 pint claret	2 oz chopped walnuts
¼ oz powdered gelatine	2 oz stem ginger, chopped
5 fl oz double cream	2 oz glacé cherries
1 tbsp castor sugar	

Stir the gelatine into a tablespoon of the wine and then dissolve by heating the wine in a cup standing in a bowl of simmering water, then blend this with the rest of the claret. Take a straight-sided glass bowl, and pour enough of the wine jelly into it to cover the bottom. Put to set in the fridge. Stand the rest in a bowl in hot water to keep from setting.

Fill a straight-sided glass with ice and stand this on top of the jelly layer in the straight-sided bowl. Pour the rest of the liquid jelly around the glass and allow to set in the fridge.

Whip the cream and blend in the sugar, chopped nuts, ginger and glacé cherries. When the jelly has set, remove the glass by taking out the ice, filling it with some warm water and then carefully lifting it out. Fill the space with the cream and fruit mixture. Chill again.

To serve, stand the bowl in some hot water for a moment until the jelly has loosened at the sides. Turn out carefully onto a chilled plate. The effect is really quite stunning.

MIDSUMMER FROTH

½ lb redcurrants	2 large egg whites
½ lb raspberries	A pinch of salt
¼ lb icing sugar	5 fl oz double cream

Purée the fruits by pressing them through a fine sieve. Don't put them into a food processor or liquidiser. This may take a little time, but it is the only way to make a successful Froth. Blend the icing sugar into the purée and leave to stand.

Whisk the egg whites until they peak and add the pinch of salt. Fold gently into the purée and then pour into a large saucepan. Using a hand whisk beat the mixture continually over a gentle heat until it begins to rise like a soufflé.

Place a spoonful of cream at the bottom of individual wine-glasses and pour the mixture on the top. Serve immediately.

HAZELNUT AND WALNUT DESSERT

4 large eggs	3 oz ground walnuts
6 oz light muscavado sugar	3 oz ground hazelnuts
FOR THE FILLING	
2 egg whites	Grated rind of 1 lemon
6 oz icing sugar	6 oz butter

Preheat the oven to gas mark 4, 350°F (180°C). Separate the eggs and beat the yolks with the sugar until they are thick and creamy. Fold in the nuts. Whisk the egg whites until they are really stiff, and fold onto the mixture.

Butter three 8-inch flan cases. Divide the mixture between each and bake in the oven for about 30 minutes. Allow to cool a little before turning out onto a wire tray.

Make the filling. Whisk the egg whites and the icing sugar in a bowl over some hot water until very thick. Blend the lemon rind into the butter, and then blend this into the egg whites.

Spread one of the nut layers with the butter cream filling, place a second layer on top, and spread over more of the filling. Top with the last layer, and decorate with more of the butter cream and with whole hazelnuts and walnuts.

AUTUMN PUDDING

1 lb Bramley or other cooking apples	1 dsp gelatine powder
12 oz blackberries	½ large white loaf, sliced
6 oz golden granulated sugar	Double cream to pour over
¼ pint water	

Peel and slice the apples into a thick saucepan and add the blackberries with the sugar and half the water. Cover tightly and cook until tender. In the remaining water dissolve the gelatine and add to the fruit mixture.

Line a 1½-pint glass pudding basin with the bread, reserving some for a lid. Pour the apple and blackberry mixture into the middle and put on the bread lid. Place a saucer and a heavy weight on top and place in the refrigerator to chill and set overnight.

Turn out onto a plate and pour over some double cream.

ST CLEMENT'S FLAN

1 large pink grapefruit	1 large orange
FOR THE FLAN CASE	
2 eggs	2 oz plain flour
2 oz castor sugar	
FOR THE LEMON CURD	
2 oz butter	1 egg
4 oz castor sugar	Juice of 1 large lemon

Make the flan case. Beat together the eggs and the sugar until they are light and creamy. Sieve in the plain flour. Spoon the mixture into a greased 7-inch flan tin and bake in the oven for 10 minutes at gas mark 4, 350°F (180°C). When cooked, allow to cool a little in the tin before turning out onto a wire tray.

You will need a double pan to make the lemon curd. Gently heat the butter and the sugar in the pan together, making sure the butter does not turn to oil. Beat together the egg and the lemon juice and slowly add to the pan. Stir gently all the time until the curd thickens. Stand it to one side and allow to cool.

When the flan case is cool spread the cooled lemon curd mixture over the bottom. Arrange segments of orange and grapefruit on the lemon curd, and serve well chilled.

APPLE AND ORANGE FLAN

1 lb cooking apples, grated	4 oz castor sugar
Juice of 1 large orange	¼ tsp cinnamon
2 eggs, beaten	8 oz shortcrust pastry

Preheat the oven to gas mark 5, 375°F (190°C). Grate the apples into a bowl, and quickly squeeze on the orange juice and stir in the eggs. Add the sugar and cinnamon and stir again.

Line a 9-inch flan tin with pastry. Pour in the filling and bake in the oven for 30 to 35 minutes.

Allow to cool and decorate with twirls of whipped double cream.

LANCASTER LEMON TART

4 oz shortcrust pastry	4 oz self-raising flour
3 tbsp lemon curd	1 oz ground almonds
3 oz butter	1 large lemon
3 oz castor sugar	1 oz flaked almonds
1 egg	

Line an 8-inch tin with the shortcrust pastry and spread the lemon curd over the base. Preheat the oven to gas mark 5, 375°F (190°C).

Cream the butter and sugar together and gradually beat in the egg. Fold in the flour and the ground almonds, and add the grated rind of the lemon with the juice. Blend together well. Spread the mixture evenly over the lemon curd and sprinkle the top with the flaked almonds.

Bake in the centre of the preheated oven for 15 minutes, then turn the temperature down to gas mark 2, 300°F (150°C) for 25 minutes. Allow to cool, and serve cold with cream.

CHOCOLATE CRUNCH BRANDY CAKE

4 oz plain chocolate	4 oz buttercrunch or ginger biscuits
4 oz unsalted butter	4 oz raisins
1 egg	2 oz glacé cherries, chopped
2 tbsp double cream	2 oz almonds, chopped
3 tbsp brandy	

In a double boiler melt the chocolate and beat in the butter, the egg, double cream and brandy. Crush the biscuits and mix with the raisins, cherries and nuts in a large bowl. Add to the chocolate mixture and then spoon into a 7-inch greased cake tin and allow to cool.

Serve with fresh double cream.

RASPBERRY CREAM PIE

8 oz shortcrust pastry	5 oz castor sugar
1 tbsp cornflour	Grated rind of 1 lemon
½ pint milk	8 oz raspberries
2 eggs, separated	

Line an 8-inch flan tin with the pastry and bake blind.

Blend the cornflour with the milk, and heat. Beat in the egg yolks, blended with 1 ounce of the sugar and the grated lemon rind, to make a custard. Cook a little more, but do not allow to boil.

Whisk the egg whites. Fold in the rest of the sugar to make a meringue mixture.

Cover the bottom of the flan case with the raspberries. Pour the custard mixture over and fold the meringue mixture on the top. Pop into a hot oven set at gas mark 7, 425°F (220°C) until the meringue browns, and serve immediately.

BAKEWELL TART

1 × 8 oz pkt puff pastry	3 large eggs
2 tbsp raspberry jam	½ tsp almond essence
4 oz butter	4 oz ground almonds
4 oz castor sugar	

Preheat the oven to gas mark 8, 450°F (230°C). Roll the pastry out to fit a 9-inch flan dish. Spread the bottom generously with the raspberry jam.

Cream the butter and sugar together, beat in the eggs and add the almond essence. Stir in the ground almonds and spoon the mixture over the jam.

Bake in the centre of the preheated oven for 5 minutes, and then turn the oven down to gas mark 2, 300°F (150°C) and cook for a further 45 minutes.

HOT FAVOURITES

HONEYED PEARS

8 English pears	*2 tbsp melted butter*
1 oz butter	*3 tbsp lime juice*
8 tbsp clear honey	*Cinnamon*

Choose underripe pears. Peel and quarter them. Grease a shallow ovenproof dish with the ounce of butter and add the pears. Mix together the honey, melted butter and lime juice and pour over. Sprinkle with the cinnamon.

Bake in the oven at gas mark 4, 350°F (180°C) for 20 minutes. Serve hot.

THE CURATE'S SPECIAL
BREAD AND BUTTER PUDDING

2 oz butter	*2 large eggs*
6 slices white bread	*1 oz castor sugar*
4 oz mixed dried fruit	*½ tsp vanilla essence*
2 oz candied cherries	*¾ pint milk*
2 oz chopped nuts	*½ oz demerara sugar*

Preheat the oven to gas mark 5, 375°F (190°C). Butter a fireproof dish well with half the butter. Spread the rest of the butter on the bread, being really generous. (If you need to use a little more, don't worry – no one's looking.) Place one layer of bread and butter on the bottom of the dish and sprinkle with some of the dried fruit, candied cherries and chopped nuts, then place another layer of bread on top, and so on, ending up with a layer of bread and butter, buttered side down.

Whisk the eggs with the castor sugar and vanilla essence. Heat the milk, but do not let it boil, and stir into the egg mixture. Pour this mixture over the bread and butter. Dot the top of the bread with a little bit more butter and sprinkle with the demerara sugar.

Bake in the oven for 45 minutes, and serve hot from the oven.

PEACH AND APRICOT MERINGUE

8 oz dried apricots	1 oz butter
1 cinnamon stick	3 egg whites
6 peaches	4 oz castor sugar

Soak the dried apricots overnight with the cinnamon stick. Next day simmer them gently for about 1 hour. Dip each of the peaches into boiling water for a minute to loosen the skins so that you can easily rub them away. Slice the peaches. Butter a shallow round oven dish and place the peaches and apricots in it. Preheat the oven to gas mark 3, 325°F (170°C).

Whisk the egg whites until they peak, whisk in half the sugar and then fold in the remaining sugar. Spoon the meringue mixture on top of the fruit, making sure that you seal the edges of the dish with the meringue.

Bake in the centre of the oven for about 30 minutes until golden brown. Serve immediately.

EVE'S PUDDING . . .
as Aunt Agatha makes it

1½ lb cooking apples, sliced	4 oz self-raising flour
5 oz butter	2 oz ground almonds
6 oz demerara sugar	½ tsp almond essence
1 tsp ground cinnamon	2 tbsp milk
2 large eggs	

Preheat the oven to gas mark 4, 350°F (180°C). Place the apples in an ovenproof dish with 1 ounce of the butter and sprinkle with 2 ounces of the demerara sugar and the ground cinnamon.

Cream the remaining butter and sugar together and gradually beat in the eggs. Mix together the flour and the ground almonds and beat into the mixture. Add the almond essence and a little milk.

Spoon the mixture over the apples and bake in the oven for 40 minutes. Serve with thick double cream.

PEACH DELIGHT

4 large peaches	4 oz demerara sugar
4 oz almond paste	1 beaten egg
12 oz puff pastry	

Preheat the oven to gas mark 7, 425°F (220°C). Cut each peach in half and remove the stones. Roll a little of the almond paste into a ball and push into the cavity in the centre of the peach. Press the 2 halves of the peach gently together.

Roll out the puff pastry and make 4 squares, each big enough to hold one of the peaches. Place a peach in the centre of each square and sprinkle with demerara sugar. Dampen the edges of the pastry with a little of the beaten egg, and bring the corners together. Seal the edges.

Brush with the beaten egg and bake in the oven for 25 minutes. Serve with double cream.

CRISPY APPLE AMBER

1½ lb cooking apples, sliced	4 oz butter
4 oz demerara sugar	1 level tsp mixed spice
4 tbsp water	2 large eggs
6 slices white bread	3 oz castor sugar

Cook the apples with the demerara sugar and water, leaving the pan uncovered so that some of the juice will evaporate. Remove from the heat and allow to cool before beating in the egg yolks. Preheat the oven to gas mark 4, 350°F (180°C).

Remove the crusts from the bread and cut the slices into triangular shapes. Melt the butter and sprinkle the mixed spice in it. Dip each side of the triangles in the melted butter and arrange them around the sides of a shallow pie dish, overlapping each one as you go round the dish.

Spoon the apple mixture into the middle of the dish. Whip the egg whites until they are really stiff and fold in the castor sugar a little at a time. Pile this meringue mixture on top of the apple and bake in the oven for 35 to 40 minutes until the meringue begins to brown.

Eat warm with cream.

BAKED LEMON PUDDING

2 oz butter	2 eggs, separated
3 oz castor sugar	1 level tbsp flour
Juice and grated rind of 1 lemon	7½ fl oz milk

Preheat the oven to gas mark 4, 350°F (180°C). Cream together the butter and sugar thoroughly. Blend in the finely grated rind of the lemon and beat again until the mixture is really fluffy. Beat the egg yolks, flour, lemon juice and milk into the mixture, which should curdle.

Whisk the egg whites until they are stiff and fold them into the mixture. Pour into a greased ovenproof dish and bake in the centre of the oven for 45 minutes until the pudding is well risen and firm on the top.

During the cooking process the mixture will separate, to form a delicious lemon base and a light, airy top.

BAKED ROLY POLY PUDDING

2 oz self-raising flour	2 eggs
6 oz castor sugar	1 tbsp milk
6 oz suet	8 oz strawberry or raspberry jam
A pinch of salt	1 beaten egg for glazing

Preheat the oven to gas mark 5, 375°F (190°C).

Sift the flour into a large mixing bowl. Use a fork to stir in the sugar, suet and pinch of salt. Beat the 2 eggs together with the milk and gradually add to the flour, sugar and suet until you have a lightish dough.

Roll the mixture out into a rectangle and smother three-quarters of it with the jam, then roll up like a swiss roll. Place on a baking sheet and brush with the beaten egg.

Bake in the oven for 40 minutes. Serve with custard.

ADAM'S APPLES

4 large cooking apples	*4 oz currants*
2 oz butter	*Ground cloves*
4 oz demerara sugar	

Preheat the oven to gas mark 5, 375°F (190°C).

Core the apples, using a very sharp knife, but leave unpeeled. Stand on a baking tray or dish and spoon alternate layers of butter, sugar and currants into the centre holes with a single pinch only of ground cloves (you don't want to overwhelm the flavour). Score a line round the 'waist' of the apples. Bake in the oven for 40 minutes.

APPLE PIE

FOR THE PASTRY	
6 oz butter	*3 tbsp chilled water*
12 oz self-raising flour	*1 beaten egg for glazing*
A pinch of salt	*A little castor sugar*

FOR THE FILLING	
1 lb Bramley cooking apples	*½ tsp cinnamon*
4 oz sultanas	*2 oz demerara sugar*

Preheat the oven to gas mark 5, 375°F (190°C).

Make the pastry. Rub the butter into the flour with the pinch of salt. Work in the water to make a dough. Divide into 2, and line a 9-inch pie plate with half the pastry.

Peel the apples and slice them onto the pastry layer. Sprinkle with the sultanas, cinnamon and demerara sugar.

Roll out the other half of the pastry and brush the edges with the beaten egg. Place on top of the apples, and press the edges down well. Make a couple of holes in the top of the pie, brush with the beaten egg and sprinkle with castor sugar. Bake in the oven for about 35 minutes. Serve with double cream.

YORKSHIRE CURD TART

2 oz butter	2 oz currants
2 oz castor sugar	Grated rind of 1 lemon
1 egg, beaten	A pinch of nutmeg
4 oz cottage cheese	6 oz shortcrust pastry

Preheat the oven to gas mark 5, 375°F (190°C). Cream the butter and sugar together and add the rest of the ingredients, mixing well as you go.

Line a 7-inch loose-bottomed flan dish with the pastry and pour the filling in. Bake in the oven for 30 to 40 minutes. Serve warm.

EYEMOUTH TART

8 oz shortcrust pastry	1 oz castor sugar
2 oz roughly chopped walnuts	1 egg, beaten
2 oz currants	1 oz melted butter
2 oz desiccated coconut	8 oz icing sugar
2 oz glacé cherries	2 tbsp lemon juice
2 oz raisins	

Preheat the oven to gas mark 5, 375°F (190°C). Roll out the pastry to line a swiss roll tin. Mix together all the dry ingredients and add the beaten egg and melted butter. Spread the mixture over the pastry and bake in the centre of the oven until golden brown, about 25 minutes.

Mix the icing sugar with the lemon juice, being careful not to add too much juice. Pour it over the tart whilst it is still hot. Serve warm with a little cream.

FIGGY TART

12 oz dried figs	½ tsp mixed spice
8 oz shortcrust pastry	1 tbsp honey
1 dsp cornflour	2 oz currants

Soak the dried figs for 12 hours and then bring to the boil and simmer for 20 minutes. Preheat the oven to gas mark 6, 400°F (200°C).

Roll out the pastry to cover a 9-inch shallow round pie dish. Drain the figs, reserving the liquid, and arrange the figs on the pastry.

Mix the cornflour with the reserved liquid and gradually bring to the boil to thicken the sauce. Add the mixed spice and the honey, and stir well. Pour the mixture over the figs and sprinkle with the currants.

Bake in the centre of the oven for 35 minutes. Serve warm.

CHORISTERS' TREACLE TART

FOR THE PASTRY	
8 oz self-raising flour	A pinch of salt
4 oz butter	3 tbsp chilled water

FOR THE FILLING	
4 tbsp syrup	4 heaped tbsp crushed ginger biscuits
½ oz unsalted butter	Grated rind of 1 lemon

Preheat the oven to gas mark 5, 375°F (190°C). Make the pastry and line a flan dish with it. Gently heat the syrup in a pan with the knob of butter and stir in the ginger biscuit crumbs. Spoon the mixture onto the pastry case and finely grate onto it the rind of the lemon.

Bake in the oven for 30 minutes. Serve with dollops of double cream.

DATE PUDDING

8 oz self-raising flour	A pinch of salt
3 oz castor sugar	1 large egg
4 oz suet	¼ pint milk
4 oz finely chopped dates	

Sift the flour and sugar into a mixing bowl and stir in the suet, chopped dates and a pinch of salt. Beat the egg and add a little of the milk to it. Stir this into the dry ingredients to make a dough – if necessary, add a little more milk.

Butter a 2-pint pudding basin and spoon in the mixture. Cover with some greaseproof paper and wrap the basin in a cloth. Steam for 1½ hours. Serve with custard.

CUMBERLAND STEAMED PUDDING

½ oz butter	4 oz suet
6 oz self-raising flour	3 eggs, beaten
6 oz cooking apples, sliced	Nutmeg
4 oz currants	Salt

Grease a 2-pint basin with the butter. Mix together all the other ingredients in a large bowl. Spoon the pudding mixture into the basin, cover with greaseproof paper and then tie with a cloth or pleated foil cover over that. Boil for 2 hours. Turn out immediately and serve with custard.

CHRISTMAS PUDDING

1 lb suet	1 large Bramley apple, grated
1 lb breadcrumbs	2 carrots, grated
1 lb currants	8 eggs, beaten
1 lb sultanas	1 tbsp gravy browning
1 lb raisins	1 small bottle stout
8 oz self-raising flour	1 wineglass brandy
4 oz glacé cherries	1 tsp salt
4 oz mixed peel	1 tsp mixed spice
4 oz chopped almonds	1 tsp nutmeg

In a large bowl mix all the dry ingredients together. Grate in the apple and carrots. Add the beaten eggs, gravy browning, stout and brandy, season with the salt and spices, and mix well. Cover and leave overnight. If it looks and feels too dry in the morning, add a little more stout.

Divide the mixture between as many basins of whatever size you require. Cover with greaseproof paper and wrap with cloth. Steam for 8 hours each.

On Christmas night, steam the pudding for 4 hours – and don't forget the sprig of holly.

CHESTER PUDDING

4 oz self-raising flour	*Salt*
4 oz shredded suet	*6 oz blackcurrant jam*
4 oz breadcrumbs	*5 tbsp milk*
2 oz castor sugar	*1 level tbsp bicarbonate of soda*

Mix together the flour, suet, breadcrumbs, sugar and salt. Make a well in the centre and add 4 ounces of the jam. Heat the milk through, but do not let it come to the boil, and stir in the bicarbonate of soda. Pour this onto the mixture in the bowl and stir well. The result will be something similar to dark blue mud! Do not worry, however, as it will turn brown in cooking.

Place the mixture in a 2-pint pudding bowl, cover with pleated foil, and steam for 3 hours in a pan of simmering water. Add hot water to top it up as necessary – do not let the pan boil dry.

When ready, turn the pudding out onto a hot dish. Melt the remaining 2 ounces of blackcurrant jam with 2 tablespoons of water and pour over the pudding. Serve with custard or cream!

SUMMER PIE

FOR THE PASTRY

8 oz flour	*2 oz castor sugar*
4 oz butter	*A little water*

FOR THE FILLING

8 oz cherries, stoned	*8 oz golden granulated sugar*
8 oz gooseberries	*Milk for glazing*
8 oz redcurrants	*1 tsp castor sugar*

Make the pastry in the usual way in the food processor. Roll out and line a 2-pint pie dish with it, leaving some aside for the lid. Preheat the oven to gas mark 4, 350°F (180°C).

Fill the pie dish with alternate layers of the washed fruits and sugar until all are used up. Top with the pastry lid, seal the edges well, glaze with a little milk and sprinkle with the castor sugar.

Bake in the centre of the preheated oven for 15 minutes, and then turn the temperature down to gas mark 3, 325°F (170°C) and cook for a further 25 to 35 minutes. Serve hot with fresh double cream.

THE BAKER'S
OVEN

It's a heartfelt belief of mine that one of the greatest pleasures in life is to be had from making cakes and baking bread. You only have to look at the produce stall at the church fête to see how many people still enjoy following the traditional recipes, and how many people still enjoy eating them. In the old days in many parts of the country – especially the north – baking day was observed as a fixed day in the weekly routine, just as wash day was, when the kitchen would fill with good smells, and batches of buns, pastries, cakes and biscuits straight out of the oven stood cheek by jowl with the freshly baked loaves of bread. Each family had its favourites, just as each region had its local speciality. It's surprising how many of these varieties still remain – lardy cake in Oxfordshire, parkin in Yorkshire, bannocks in Scotland.

With so many people out at work all day, teatime with its traditional spread of scones and buttered bread, as well as sponge cakes, chocolate cakes, iced cakes and fruit cakes, does not feature very much in our lives any more. But most people are able at some point in the day to squeeze in a slice of cake – and don't forget that a good cake can be stored in an airtight tin and brought out when wanted. In fact, many fruit cakes *improve* with keeping in a tin. So if you have time during the week to fit in a little baking, it's worth making a batch and keeping some for later.

One tip when baking cakes is to try and beat in a lot of air so that they will rise. But mind you, there's always the converse danger that you will overbeat them and force all the air out – so that they do not rise at all. Cake making is one area of cooking where I think it is vitally important to follow the recipe to the letter. One thing that can cause problems is your oven – every oven has its whims, either running too hot or too cold, and the safest bet to ensure you achieve perfect results is to invest in an oven thermometer. But cake making really is not difficult, and it should always be fun. The recipes I've chosen here are ones that I think will work even for beginners.

I've also included a couple of bread recipes, and this is one area where a revolution has taken place in our national eating habits as more and more people have turned away from eating steambaked cotton wool to demand different kinds of tastier, healthier bread. What greater satisfaction can there be than biting into a crusty, chewy slice of bread from a loaf that you have baked yourself? Just try it.

GRANTHAM GINGERBREAD BISCUITS

8 oz flour	1 tsp ground ginger
8 oz castor sugar	4 oz butter
½ tsp baking powder	1 egg, beaten

Preheat the oven to gas mark 4, 350°F (180°C). Sift together the flour, sugar, baking powder and ginger. Soften the butter and work it into the flour mixture with the egg.

Mix well by hand and roll the dough into pieces the size of a walnut. Place them well apart on a floured baking tray and bake for 30 minutes, keeping a careful eye on them so that they do not brown.

BAXI BUNS

2 eggs	2 oz sultanas
The weight of the eggs in butter and wholemeal flour	1 tsp each of ginger, cinnamon and nutmeg
1 oz castor sugar	1 heaped tsp baking powder

Preheat the oven to gas mark 5, 375°F (190°C). Put everything except the sultanas into the mixing bowl of a food mixer or food processor and process for a couple of minutes. Mix in the sultanas by hand.

Spoon into 10 or 12 baking cases and cook for 10 or 12 minutes until firm and brown. Serve with a freshly brewed pot of tea!

COVENTRY GOD CAKES

2 oz butter	1 tsp cinnamon
1 tbsp honey	1 tbsp rum
6 oz currants	1 lb puff pastry
1 oz demerara sugar	1 beaten egg
4 oz mixed peel	1 oz castor sugar
1 tsp mixed spice	

Preheat the oven to gas mark 7, 425°F (220°C). Melt the butter in a pan and stir in the honey, currants, sugar, mixed peel, spices and rum. Mix well and then stand to one side.

Roll out the pastry into 6-inch squares (you'll probably have enough for 6). Divide the mixture between the squares and dampen the edges of each pastry square with a little egg. Fold the pastry across the diagonal to make a triangle and seal the edges well. Glaze the top with the beaten egg and dredge with the castor sugar. Bake in the oven for 10 to 15 minutes until well browned and puffed up.

ANGEL CAKE

10 egg whites	10 oz castor sugar
4 oz plain flour	1 tsp vanilla essence
1 tsp cream of tartar	A pinch of salt
FOR THE ICING	
4 oz icing sugar	A drop of almond essence
2 tbsp boiling water	

Preheat the oven to gas mark 4, 350°F (180°C). Beat the egg whites until they are very stiff – so stiff, in fact, that they can support 2 whole eggs. Sift the flour with the cream of tartar 4 times, and then sift in the sugar 4 times. Add the flour and sugar very gradually to the egg whites, folding in with great care. Lastly add the vanilla essence and the salt.

Spoon the cake mixture into a ring tin and bake in the oven for 45 minutes. Turn out onto a wire tray. When cool, make an icing of icing sugar and water flavoured with a little almond essence and cover the cake with it.

PINEAPPLE FRUIT CAKE

4 oz butter	6 oz light muscavado sugar
1 small tin crushed pineapple	2 eggs
12 oz mixed dried fruit	8 oz self-raising flour
4 oz glacé cherries	

Preheat the oven to gas mark 2, 300°F (150°C). Melt the butter in a thick saucepan and then stir in all the fruit and the sugar. Remove the pan from the heat and add the eggs one at a time, stirring well. Finally add the flour.

Turn into an 8-inch cake tin and bake in the oven for 1 hour. Leave to cool, turn out of tin and dry on a rack.

COFFEE WALNUT CAKE

6 oz light muscavado sugar	1 tsp baking powder
6 oz butter	4 oz glacé cherries
2 eggs	4 oz chopped walnuts
6 oz plain flour	
FOR THE FILLING	
2 oz butter	1 tbsp coffee essence
6 oz icing sugar	
FOR THE TOPPING	
4 oz icing sugar	1 tbsp coffee essence
A little water	Walnuts to decorate

Preheat the oven to gas mark 4, 350°F (180°C). Cream the sugar and the butter together and beat in the eggs. Add the flour and the rest of the ingredients. Grease a 7-inch cake tin and spoon in the mixture. Cook for 1 hour. Allow to cool in the tin for 15 minutes before turning out onto a wire rack.

For the filling blend together the butter and icing sugar and add the coffee essence. Split the cooled cake very carefully and spread the filling inside. Place the top layer on the cake.

Blend the icing sugar, water and coffee essence for the topping and spread over the cake. Arrange the walnut halves on top and serve when the vicar comes to tea.

PLAIN CAKE

6 oz self-raising flour	2 tbsp milk
2 oz ground almonds	1 tsp vanilla essence
6 oz butter	3 large eggs
6 oz castor sugar	

Preheat the oven to gas mark 4, 350°F (180°C). Weigh out all the ingredients, apart from the eggs, in the weighing pan together. Whisk the eggs together and then add the rest of the ingredients and whisk until smooth and seemingly fluffy.

Place the mixture in a greased 7-inch baking tin or in a ring tin and bake in the oven for 1 hour. Cool for 10 minutes, turn out of tin and leave to dry on the rack.

For a change, you can always try adding 2 teaspoonfuls of caraway seeds to this cake.

THE THREE 'A'S CAKE

8 oz self-raising flour	3 large eggs
6 oz castor sugar	1½ lb cooking apples, sliced
6 oz butter	3 oz apricot conserve
1 tsp almond essence	2 oz flaked almonds

Preheat the oven to gas mark 3, 325°F (170°C). Put the three 'A's of the recipe – the apples, apricot conserve and almonds – on one side for the moment, and blend together all the other ingredients to a smooth mixture, either by hand or in a processor or mixer.

Grease a loose-bottomed 8-inch cake tin well, and put in it the sliced apples so that they generously cover the base of the tin. In a thick saucepan gently heat the apricot conserve. Before it is too runny, spoon it over the sliced apples and then sprinkle half the flaked almonds over the top. Finally add the cake mixture in a layer.

Bake in the oven for 1 hour before sprinkling the rest of the flaked almonds on the top and baking for a further 30 minutes. Cool for 15 minutes and remove from tin. Leave to dry on a wire rack.

NORFOLK VINEGAR CAKE

1 lb plain flour	8 oz raisins
8 oz butter	4 fl oz milk plus 1 tbsp
8 oz granulated sugar	1 tsp bicarbonate of soda
8 oz sultanas	2 tbsp vinegar

Preheat the oven to gas mark 5, 375°F (190°C). The real essential this cake needs is lightness of touch. Rub the flour and the butter together with your fingertips. Then add the sugar and the fruit. Mix the bicarbonate of soda with the tablespoon of milk and add to the rest of the milk and the vinegar. Make a well in the centre of the dry ingredients and pour in the milk, beating well until you have a smooth texture.

Spoon the mixture into a lined 9-inch cake tin, making sure that you leave it looking like a pile of sand with a point in the middle. Cook in the oven for 1 hour 15 minutes. Leave to cool, then turn out onto rack.

DUNDEE CAKE

8 oz currants	*12 oz plain flour*
8 oz sultanas	*1 tbsp mixed spice*
8 oz raisins	*8 oz unsalted butter*
4 oz glacé cherries, halved	*8 oz light muscavado sugar*
4 oz mixed peel	*5 large eggs*
Finely grated rind of 1 large orange	*3 oz whole blanched almonds*

Preheat the oven to gas mark 2, 300°F (150°C). Mix together the dried fruits, glacé cherries, mixed peel and orange rind. Sieve together the plain flour and the mixed spice.

Cream together the butter and the muscavado sugar and beat in the eggs one at a time, adding a little of the flour after each egg. Fold in the rest of the flour and stir in the fruit a little at a time, mixing well.

Prepare an 8-inch cake tin by tying on a collar of greaseproof paper. Spoon the cake mixture into the tin and smooth the top with the back of a spoon. Arrange the whole blanched almonds around the top of the cake in rings.

Bake in the middle of the oven for 4 to 4½ hours. Leave the cake in the tin for 15 minutes before turning out and allowing to cool on a wire tray.

MINCEMEAT CAKE

1 lb mincemeat	*2 oz chopped walnuts*
8 oz wholewheat flour	*Grated zest of 1 orange and 1 lemon*
3 level tsp baking powder	*3 eggs*
5 oz dark muscavado sugar	*2 oz blanched almonds*
5 oz butter	*8 candied cherries*
6 oz mixed fruit	

Preheat the oven to gas mark 3, 325°F (170°C). An electric mixer is ideal for making this cake. Simply put all the ingredients, except the almonds and cherries, in it and mix together. Or put them all in a bowl and beat by hand.

Grease an 8-inch cake tin and spoon the mixture into it. Decorate the top with the almonds and cherries. Bake in the oven for 1 hour 20 minutes. Allow the cake to cool in the tin for 20 minutes and then turn out onto a wire rack.

SHEARING CAKE

8 oz plain flour	8 oz butter
8 oz wholemeal flour	12 oz light muscavado sugar
1 tsp baking powder	Juice and grated rind of 1 lemon
1 tsp freshly grated nutmeg	2 large eggs
1 dsp caraway seeds	½ pint milk
Salt	

Preheat the oven to gas mark 4, 350°F (180°C). In a warmed mixing bowl sieve together the flours, baking powder, nutmeg, caraway seeds and salt.

Cream together the butter and sugar and add the juice and finely grated rind of the lemon. Begin to blend in the flour and beat in the eggs one at a time, adding the milk gradually to make a good dropping mixture. Stir well until blended and creamy.

Grease a 9-inch square cake tin and pour in the mixture. Bake in the centre of the oven for 30 minutes and then turn the oven down to gas mark 2, 300°F (150°C) for a further 1½ hours. Remove from oven and leave to cool for 10 minutes. Turn onto wire rack.

This used to be made at sheep-shearing time.

PARKIN

3 oz self-raising flour	2 oz ground almonds
3 oz wholemeal flour	2 level tbsp warm syrup
4 oz demerara sugar	2 level tbsp black treacle
1 level tsp ground ginger	4 oz butter
½ tsp nutmeg	1 egg
½ tsp salt	4 tbsp milk
2 oz oatmeal	

Preheat the oven to gas mark 3, 325°F (170°C). Sift together the flours, sugar, spices and salt and then stir in the oatmeal and almonds. Melt the syrup, black treacle and the butter together, and then beat the egg and milk together. Mix all the ingredients together very thoroughly.

Turn into an 8-inch greased cake tin and bake in the centre of the oven for 1 to 1½ hours. Cool in tin for 15 minutes and turn onto rack.

SIMNEL CAKE

6 oz butter	1 tsp cinnamon
6 oz light muscavado sugar	1 tsp nutmeg
3 large eggs, beaten	3 tbsp milk
12 oz currants	1 lb almond paste
4 oz sultanas	2 tbsp apricot jam
4 oz mixed peel	Beaten egg for glazing
8 oz plain flour	

Preheat the oven to gas mark 2, 300°F (150°C). Cream together the butter and the sugar. Add the beaten eggs and then the rest of the ingredients, except the almond paste and apricot jam.

Grease a 7-inch cake tin. Place half the cake mixture in the tin. Roll out half the almond paste into a flat saucer shape to fit the tin, and place over the cake mixture. Spoon on the rest of the cake mixture and smooth the top.

Bake the cake in the oven for 2 to 2½ hours. Allow the cake to cool in the tin and then turn out. Glaze the top of the cake with a little apricot jam and roll out the rest of the almond paste to cover the cake. Lay on top and trim. Make 11 balls with any remaining almond paste and arrange on top of the cake in a circle. Brush with a little beaten egg and brown under the grill for a moment.

The balls traditionally represent the apostles, minus Judas Iscariot, and the cake was made for Easter or, sometimes, Mothering Sunday.

HEREFORD CIDER CAKE

8 oz self-raising flour	4 oz butter
4 oz castor sugar	2 eggs
1 level tsp bicarbonate of soda	7 fl oz sweet cider
2 level tsp ground ginger	

Preheat the oven to gas mark 4, 350°F (180°C). Mix all the dry ingredients together and then rub the butter in by hand. Beat the eggs and cider together and gradually pour in to the mixture, mixing in well with a fork. Turn into a greased 2-lb loaf tin and bake for 1 hour. Cool in tin for 15 minutes and turn onto rack.

LINCOLNSHIRE PLUM BREAD

8 oz butter	1 tsp mixed spice
8 oz light muscavado sugar	1 oz chopped walnuts
1 lb self-raising flour	A pinch of salt
12 oz currants	4 large eggs, beaten
12 oz sultanas	4 tbsp milk
2 oz glacé cherries	

Preheat the oven to gas mark 5, 375°F (190°C). Cream the butter and the sugar together and blend in the rest of the ingredients, gradually adding the milk as necessary. Grease a couple of 1-lb loaf tins and divide the mixture between them. Bake in the centre of the oven for 1½ hours. Leave to cool in the tins, then dry on a wire rack.

This is best kept in an airtight tin and served at teatime the next day sliced and spread with butter.

BURFORD LARDY CAKE

1 lb plain flour	6 oz lard
½ oz salt	4 oz demerara sugar
½ oz fresh yeast	3 oz sultanas
1 tsp sugar	2 oz currants
½ pint warm water	

Sieve the flour into a warm bowl and sprinkle in the salt. Make a well in the centre of the flour. Sprinkle the yeast into the warm water with the teaspoonful of sugar and allow to become frothy. Pour this mixture into the well together with 2 ounces of the lard, and mix into a dough. Knead well.

Allow the dough to rise and then roll out into a rectangle on a floured board. Spread about one third of the remaining lard, the demerara sugar, sultanas and currants over two-thirds of the surface of the dough and fold. Half turn the dough on the board, and roll out again. Repeat the process twice more.

Roll the dough out again, then roll up like a swiss roll and cut in half and place each half in a 6-inch cake tin to make 2 loaves. Allow to rise. Cover with a clean towel and store in a warm place.

Preheat the oven to gas mark 6, 400°F (200°C) and bake for 45 minutes. Serve just warm.

BATH BUNS

1/2 oz fresh yeast	4 oz butter
1 tsp castor sugar	2 oz sultanas
1/4 pint milk, warmed	4 oz candied peel
1 lb plain bread-making flour	2 oz castor sugar
A pinch of salt	3 large eggs

Start the yeast working by blending it with the sugar and warmed milk and allowing to stand covered in a warm place until it becomes frothy.

Place 8 ounces of the flour in a warmed mixing bowl with the salt. Make a well in the centre of the flour and stir in the yeast mixture. Cover and leave to work in a warm place for about 1 hour.

Rub the butter into the remaining flour until you have a consistency like breadcrumbs. Stir in the sultanas, candied peel, sugar and the yeast–flour mixture. Beat in the eggs one at a time to make a sturdy dough. Place in a greased bowl and cover. Let it stand in a warm place until well risen (this will probably take 1 or 2 hours or, if you wish, you can leave it overnight).

Form the dough into small bun shapes and place on a greased baking tray, well apart. Sprinkle with some crushed sugar cubes and leave to prove for 2 hours. Preheat the oven to gas mark 7, 425°F (220°C) and bake for 15 to 20 minutes.

HOT CROSS BUNS

1 pkt dried yeast	6 oz currants
1/2 pint milk and water mixed and warmed	3 oz mixed peel
	1/2 tsp cinnamon
1 tsp sugar	1/2 tsp nutmeg
1 lb strong white flour	1/2 tsp mixed spice
1 tsp salt	Shortcrust pastry for the crosses
2 oz butter	

Mix the yeast in the milk and water with the teaspoon of sugar. Leave for 20 minutes. In a warmed bowl mix all the ingredients together by hand. Knead well and form a firm dough. Place in a large warmed bowl, covered, and allow to rise and double its bulk.

Turn the dough out and knead again. Divide into 12 small balls and allow to rise in a warm place. Make crosses on the top with some thin pastry strips held in place with beaten egg. Preheat the oven to gas mark 6, 400°F (200°C) and bake for 15 to 20 minutes. Baste with a sugar–water solution once or twice during baking to make a lovely sticky crust. Serve slightly warm with plenty of butter!

CHELSEA BUNS

8 oz plain flour	¼ pint warmed milk
½ tsp salt	2 oz chopped peel
2 oz butter	2 oz sultanas
½ oz fresh yeast	2 oz currants
2 oz castor sugar	1 egg white
1 egg	1 oz castor sugar for glazing

Sift the flour and the salt together and rub in 1 ounce of the butter. Blend the yeast and 1 ounce of the sugar together, beat the egg and warmed milk together, and pour over the yeast. Pour the mixture into the flour and knead well. Cover and leave in a warm place to double in bulk.

Turn out onto a floured board and knead well. Roll out into an oblong. Spread the remaining butter on two-thirds of this dough. Fold the dough into 3, folding in the end that isn't buttered first, half turn and roll out again. Spread the dough with half the fruit and half the remaining sugar, and fold over again. Half turn, roll out again, and add the rest of the fruit and remaining sugar. Roll up like a swiss roll. Cut the roll into slices 1 inch thick. Place on a greased baking tray, cover and leave to prove for about 30 minutes in a warm place.

Preheat the oven to gas mark 6, 400°F (200°C).

Brush the slices with egg white and sprinkle with castor sugar. Bake in the oven for 20 minutes. Separate whilst hot and eat warm.

BANNOCKS

½ oz fresh yeast	1 lb plain flour
1 tsp castor sugar	1 tsp salt
½ pint milk	4 oz sultanas
1 oz butter	2 oz candied peel
1 egg yolk	

Blend the yeast and the sugar together. Warm the milk and melt the butter in it. Pour over the yeast and sugar. Leave in a warm place for 25 minutes. Beat the egg yolk and add to the yeast mixture. Stir in the flour and the salt to make a dough. Cover and leave in a warm place to double in size. In the meantime, mix the sultanas and candied peel together.

Remove the dough to a floured board and knead well, working in the sultanas and candied peel. Keeping the board well floured, knead the dough into 4 round cakes and place on greased baking trays. Allow to rise in a warm place for about 30 minutes.

Preheat the oven to gas mark 6, 400°F (200°C) and bake for 20 minutes.

TEA CAKES

1 lb plain flour	½ oz fresh yeast
1 tsp salt	½ pint warm milk
2 oz castor sugar plus 1 tsp	4 oz currants
1 oz butter	

Sift the flour and salt together with the 2 ounces of castor sugar, and rub in the butter using your fingertips. Keep these ingredients warm. Blend together the yeast and teaspoonful of sugar and add half the warmed milk. Stand in a warm place for 20 minutes, then blend this mixture into the flour, add more milk if you need to, and beat well. Leave the dough to rise for about 1 hour. Knead on a floured board, working in the currants.

Divide into 9 slightly flattened rounds. Place on greased baking trays and leave to rise for 20 minutes. Preheat the oven to gas mark 6, 400°F (200°C) and bake for 10 minutes. Serve warm or toasted, with oodles of butter!

MILK ROLLS

¼ oz fresh yeast	12 oz plain flour
½ tsp castor sugar	½ tsp salt
8 fl oz milk, warmed	1 oz butter

First of all, get the yeast working by blending it with the sugar and dissolving in 5 fluid ounces (¼ pint) of the warmed milk. Cover and leave to stand for 20 minutes.

Warm the flour and sift it into a warmed bowl with the salt. Rub in the butter with your fingertips. Make a well in the middle of the flour and gradually add the yeast mixture, stirring in more warmed milk as necessary to make a soft dough. Knead well and leave in a warm place to double in size.

Knead again, and then divide into little rolls or shapes like twists and fingers. Place on a greased baking tray and allow to rise for about 30 minutes. Preheat the oven to gas mark 7, 425°F (220°C). Brush the rolls with a little warmed milk and bake in the oven for 15 minutes.

BROWN BREAD

1 oz fresh yeast	2 tsp salt
¼ pint warm water	1 tsp sugar
1 dsp vegetable oil	2 oz bran
12 oz wholemeal flour	1 tbsp wheatgerm
12 oz strong plain flour	

Crumble the yeast into the warmed water in a warm bowl and mix until the yeast has dissolved. Gently stir in the oil. Mix all the rest of the ingredients together and add to the liquid, mixing well until the sides of the bowl are left clean. Remember to work fast and keep things warm. Turn the dough out onto a floured board and knead well.

Place the mixture in a greased bowl, cover, and leave to rise until doubled in bulk. Knead again. Grease a couple of 2-lb loaf tins and divide the dough between them. Cover and allow to rise again until the dough appears over the top of the tins. Preheat the oven to gas mark 6, 400°F (200°C) and bake for 35 to 40 minutes. Leave to cool in tins, then turn out onto a wire rack to dry.

SODA BREAD

1 lb plain flour	1 heaped tsp cream of tartar
1 tsp salt	1 oz butter
1 level tsp bicarbonate of soda	½ pint milk

Preheat the oven to gas mark 7, 425°F (220°C). Mix all the dry ingredients together and rub in the butter with your fingertips. Mix in the milk until you get a soft dough. Knead lightly and flatten into a large round cake. Make a large cross on the top. Place on a floured baking tray and bake in the oven for 30 minutes.

A useful bread if you run out and have no yeast in the house.

A PRETTY
PICKLE

For some reason, many of us confine our eating of pickles and chutneys to the Christmas season when we enjoy a tangy piccalilli or a sweet and sour fruit chutney with the cold turkey and ham on Boxing Day – and forget about them for the rest of the year. Really, we have little cause to do this, for pickles go so well with so many things – cheese (where would the ploughman's lunch be without pickled onion?), cold meats, savoury pies, sausages, scotch eggs, hamburgers and grilled meats . . . the list is endless. And of course they make an ideal accompaniment to curries and other spicy dishes. A little pickle between two slices of cheese in a toasted cheese sandwich must be reckoned one of the supreme pleasures of life.

It's a mistake, too, to restrict our enjoyment of pickles only to the well-known brand varieties, for they are so easy and satisfying to make. All that chopping and simmering can be very calming and relaxing amid the normal rush of life, and conducive to peaceful meditation. You'll find it usually becomes a solitary pastime anyway, since the smell of cooking vinegar will drive most people out of your kitchen! Don't worry, though – the smell bears absolutely no relation to the end result. Chutneys and pickles always improve with keeping, but never keep them for more than 2 years! You'll find there are various kinds of white preserving vinegars available, but I find ordinary brown malt vinegar does just as well.

Like other areas of home cooking – baking, for example – favourite tried and tested recipes tend to be hoarded and passed down through families. Over the years friends and parishioners have given them to me, and the ones I have included here are my own favourites, the ones I find I keep going back to every year when pickling time comes round again. . . .

KENDAL DAMSON PICKLE

3 lb best damsons	12 coriander seeds
3 lb golden granulated sugar	¾ pint malt vinegar
24 cloves	1 chilli per jar

Choose freshly picked, dark, ripe damsons. Wash them well and allow them to drain. Add the sugar, cloves and coriander seeds to the vinegar in a saucepan. Bring slowly to the boil and simmer for 10 minutes. Pour the vinegar mixture over the damsons and leave for 24 hours.

Strain the juice into a large saucepan and then bring to the boil. Carefully lower the damsons into it and cook gently for 5 minutes. Leave the pickle to cool before pouring into jars, adding a chilli at the bottom of each one. Seal in the usual way.

This pickle needs to mature for a couple of months before using. It is delicious with cold roast pork and turkey.

MARROW CHUTNEY

4 lb marrow	1 lb small onions, finely chopped
3 oz salt	1 lb golden granulated sugar
2 lb cooking apples, chopped	2¾ pints malt vinegar
8 oz dried apricots, chopped	3 level tsp ground ginger
4 oz sultanas	

Pick a fine marrow. Peel it and cut into small pieces without removing the seeds. In a large pan, make layers of marrow, sprinkling each one with salt until all is used up. Leave to stand overnight, and in the morning drain off the juices. Wash the marrow thoroughly and allow to drain well before proceeding with the recipe.

Put the marrow, apples, apricots and sultanas in a large preserving pan and add the onions, sugar, vinegar and ginger. Cover with a tight-fitting lid. Simmer for 1 hour, stirring regularly until it has thickened to a jam consistency.

To test the flavour (which may need adjusting with the addition of a little salt) remove a little in a teaspoon, let it go cold, and taste. When you are satisfied you have the right balance, pour the mixture into warmed jars and cover in the usual way.

SPICED APPLE CHUTNEY

4 lb Bramley or other cooking apples	2½ pints vinegar
2 lb onions	2 oz mustard seed
1 clove garlic	1 oz ground ginger
4 fresh chillies	1 oz salt
1 lb sultanas	¼ tsp cayenne pepper
2 lb dark muscavado sugar	

Peel and slice the apples and onions. Place them in a large, thick preserving pan and add the rest of the ingredients. Gently bring to the boil and simmer for a couple of hours, or until the mixture easily coats the back of a wooden spoon. Allow to cool and then pour carefully into warmed preserving jars. Seal immediately.

PENELOPE'S PEACH CHUTNEY

2 lb fresh peaches	1 tbsp mustard seed
4 oz chopped onion	1 tbsp red chilli powder
1 small clove garlic, chopped	¾ lb golden granulated sugar
4 oz raisins	1 dsp salt
2 oz stem ginger, chopped	1½ pints vinegar

Peel the peaches and chop them up into fairly large chunks. Mix them with the chopped onion, garlic and raisins and place with all the other ingredients in a thick saucepan. Bring to the boil and simmer for 1 hour until the mixture is dark and thick. Pour into heated jam jars and seal immediately. Leave the pickle 1 month to mature before using.

GOOSEBERRY CHUTNEY

3 lb green gooseberries	1 oz salt
1 lb onions, chopped	1 oz ground ginger
2 pints vinegar	½ level tsp cayenne pepper
4 oz sultanas	½ oz mustard seed
8 oz raisins	¼ tsp turmeric
¾ lb demerara sugar	

Wash the gooseberries, and head and tail them. Place with all the other ingredients in a large saucepan. Cover and bring gently to the boil. Simmer for just over 1 hour, stirring regularly to prevent it sticking to the bottom, until the chutney has thickened, then pour into warmed jam jars and cover in the usual way.

LEMON CHUTNEY

4 large lemons	*4 oz seedless raisins*
1 lb onions, chopped	*½ oz mustard powder*
1 oz salt	*½ tsp cayenne pepper*
1 lb demerara sugar	*1 tsp ground ginger*
1 pint vinegar	

Do not peel the lemons, cut them into slices and remove all the pips. Mix with the chopped onion in a dish and sprinkle with the salt. Leave for 24 hours.

Drain well, then place all the ingredients in a large saucepan. Bring to the boil and simmer for 1 hour. Pour the chutney into warmed jam jars and allow to cool before sealing.

PLUM CHUTNEY

2 lb Victoria plums	*8 oz sultanas*
8 oz onion, chopped	*1 clove garlic, crushed*
1¼ pints vinegar	*2 oz salt*
2 lb demerara sugar	*1 oz stem ginger, chopped*
8 oz raisins	

Split each plum with a sharp knife and remove the stone. Put the plums with all the other ingredients in a large saucepan and bring to the boil. Allow to simmer for about an hour, stirring continually. When it has thickened remove from the heat and allow to stand for 30 minutes before pouring into warmed jam jars. Cover in the usual way.

TOMATO AND MARROW CHUTNEY

4 lb ripe tomatoes	¼ tsp of each of the following:
1 lb marrow, skinned and deseeded	paprika, cinnamon, allspice, ground
½ lb onions	cloves and ground mace
½ oz salt	¾ lb demerara sugar
	½ pint vinegar

Peel the tomatoes and chop them up. Mince the marrow with the onions and mix all the ingredients together, except the sugar and vinegar. In a thick saucepan, gently cook all the vegetables together with a very little water for 1½ hours.

Heat the vinegar just to boiling point and dissolve the sugar in it. Add to the vegetables and simmer for 20 minutes until thick. Pour into warmed jars and cover in the usual way. Delicious with pork.

RHUBARB AND ORANGE CHUTNEY

2½ lb rhubarb	2 lb demerara sugar
2 large oranges	1 lb seedless raisins
1 lb onions, finely chopped	1 tsp allspice
1½ pints vinegar	

Cut the rhubarb into 2-inch chunks and place in a large, thick saucepan. Finely grate in the rind of the oranges and then squeeze in the juice. Add the finely chopped onions and the rest of the ingredients. Bring to the boil and simmer for 1½ hours, remembering to stir occasionally.

When it has cooked and cooled a little, pour into warmed jars and seal.

PARSON'S PICCALILLI

1 large red pepper	1 head of celery
1 large green pepper	3 oz salt
2 lb green tomatoes	1½ pints malt vinegar
2 lb ripe tomatoes	1 lb golden granulated sugar
1 large onion	1 tsp mustard powder
1 cucumber	1 tsp pepper

Wash, deseed and slice the peppers. Wash and slice the tomatoes, onion, cucumber and celery. Place layers of the vegetables in a large bowl, sprinkling salt between each one, and allow to stand for at least 12 hours in a cool place. Drain the vegetables well.

Place the vegetables in a pan and add the rest of the ingredients. Bring to the boil and then allow to simmer for 1 hour. When cooked pour into warmed jars and seal immediately. Leave for 1 month before using.

CORNUCOPIA PICKLE

3 pints water	8 oz green tomatoes
8 oz salt	8 oz ridge cucumbers
8 oz pickling onions	8 oz French beans
8 oz cauliflower florets	3 pints pickling vinegar

Bring the 3 pints of water to the boil and pour onto the salt to make a strong brine solution. Allow to cool. Choose fresh, firm vegetables and wash them thoroughly. Peel the onions, quarter the tomatoes, cube the ridge cucumbers and slice the beans. Place all the vegetables in a large bowl and cover with the brine mixture. Leave to stand for 24 hours.

Drain the vegetables well and pack into screw-topped pickling jars. Cover with the vinegar. It will take about a month for the vinegar to seep gradually into all the vegetables, and so you will need to top up the jars from time to time. When you think the vegetables have drunk their fill of vinegar, put on a permanent seal and leave for a further month before using.

SWEET MUSTARD PICKLE

4 lb mixed vegetables diced very small: marrow, cauliflower, carrot, runner beans, turnip, swede	8 oz sultanas
	4 cloves
	1 cup flour
1 lb very small onions	1/2 oz turmeric
Salt	1/4 oz ground ginger
3 pints vinegar	1/2 oz mustard seed
1 lb demerara sugar	

Sprinkle all the vegetables with salt and leave overnight. Next day drain off the juice. Boil the vegetables in the vinegar with the sugar, sultanas and cloves for 30 minutes.

Mix together the flour, spices and mustard seed and blend with a little vinegar. Add to the main pan and boil for a further 30 minutes, stirring continuously until it thickens. Pour into warmed jars and cover in the usual way.

PICKLED WALNUTS

3 lb green walnuts	1/2 oz cloves
4 pints brine (see recipe)	1/2 oz allspice
2 pints vinegar	1/2 oz ground ginger
1 oz black peppercorns	1/2 oz mustard seed
1 oz white peppercorns	1 tsp salt
1/2 oz mace	

Place the green walnuts in a pan of cold water and bring them to the boil for a minute or two. Rub off their skins and then soak them in a strong brine solution (2 lbs of salt to 4 pints of water – if you can float an egg in it, it's strong enough!). Leave for 9 days or so. Remove them from the brine and stand them on a sunny windowsill until they turn black.

Now comes stage two. Boil the vinegar with the black and white peppercorns for about 10 minutes. Strain the vinegar and let it cool.

Mix all the spices together, pounding them in a pestle and mortar if necessary. Pack the walnuts into jam jars, sprinkling the mixed spices between layers. Pour the vinegar over the walnuts and seal on the lids. Store for a couple of months before using.

VINTAGE
STUFF

I've included a section on homemade drinks, alcoholic and non-alcoholic, because I think they occupy a sadly neglected corner of our national larder. After all, people have been experimenting with ways of making drinks for almost as long as they have been cooking, or perhaps even longer. Our forefathers were certainly fermenting beers and meads from various seeds and grains, and from honey, almost as soon as they had settled down to a farming life. Considering what we are prepared to pay for spirits and wines from the off-licence, and what we spend on fizzy pops and sugary drinks for our children (only to rot their teeth – see page 76), I think it is a great pity we don't do more with the traditional recipes for homemade wines and cordials that this country is so rich in. Although there will be some initial layout on winemaking equipment such as a demijohn fitted with an airlock, in the long run they'll turn out to be money-saving, I'm sure. Indeed, many of the ingredients can be grown in the garden or gathered in the hedgerows. And they are exciting and just that bit different.

Perhaps I should add a word about alcohol. It won't have escaped your notice that I'm not averse to using it, particularly in cooking – but in moderation, I must stress. I think there are times when we are all grateful for something to help us relax a little, and alcohol can do that very effectively, used wisely. But the results that can be caused by its misuse are all too frequently nothing short of tragic, affecting family and friends as well as the immediate sufferer; and many people are ill-advised to drink alcohol for medical reasons. For them, and especially children, I have included two homemade soft drinks which I think are a good deal nicer than the manufactured varieties whose discarded cans adorn our roadsides as thickly as buttercups and daisies these days.

DAMSON WINE

8 lb fresh damsons, washed and stoned	1 Camden tablet (available from chemists)
7 pints water	½ oz yeast
4 lb demerara sugar	

Place all the fruit in a large pan and crush with the end of a rolling pin. Boil 1 quart of the water and allow to go cold. Pour this onto the damsons. Crush and add the Camden tablet, mixing it into the pulp. Allow to stand, covered, for 2 hours.

Take one-third of the sugar (1 lb 5 oz) and boil it for 1 minute in 3 pints of the water. Let this cool and then add to the pulp together with the yeast and mix well. Allow to ferment for 7 days.

At the end of this period, strain the juice into a gallon demijohn and fit an airlock. Boil one-third more of the sugar with 1 pint of water and allow to cool before adding to the fermenting juice.

Rack the wine after a further 10 days' fermenting. Rack the wine again.

Boil the remaining water and sugar together and allow to cool before adding to the wine. Replace the airlock and allow the fermentation to continue until it stops! (About 3 weeks – you'll know when it stops bubbling.)

Decant, and bottle. This amount should make 4 to 5 bottles. Keep for 2 years.

DAMSON SIN GIN

2½ lb damsons	8 cloves
1 lb demerara sugar	1 bottle gin

Prick all the fruit and pack an old-fashioned sweet jar or tall lidded containers with layers of the fruit and sugar with the odd clove or two put in at random. Pour in the gin to cover, put on the lid, and leave for 6 weeks. Strain off the liqueur and decant into a bottle.

This can be served neat or with a dash of tonic water. Either way it's wonderfully warming. You can make it with sloes from hedgerows, too. If you gather them in the autumn it will be ready just in time for Christmas.

MARROW WINE

1 × 4 lb ripe marrow	3 lb demerara sugar
8 oz raisins	Juice of 1 lemon
1 gallon water	1 oz fresh yeast

Slice up and deseed the marrow but do not discard the skin. Chop up the flesh very finely and put in a large pan. Add the raisins and cold water and simmer until the marrow is tender.

Put the sugar in a large bowl and strain the marrow water onto it. Stir in the lemon juice. Allow to become lukewarm and then add the yeast. Cover and leave to stand for 4 days, stirring daily.

Strain the mixture into a demijohn and fit an airlock. Allow to ferment, feeding the wine regularly with 1 tbsp sugar every 2 or 3 weeks. Rack off the sediment, then strain again when fermentation has finished (about 3 weeks) and bottle. This should make about 4 to 5 bottles. It is best left for 2 years.

RECTORY RESTORATIVE

6 eggs, beaten	1 wineglass cognac
10 fl oz single cream	¼ tsp grated nutmeg
½ pint sherry	

Blend together the eggs and the cream. Add the sherry and brandy with the nutmeg and whisk again. Pour into some chilled bottles and store in the refrigerator, ready for use in an emergency!

CHURCHWARDEN'S CUP

2 cups demerara sugar	1 apple, sliced
½ pint boiling water	1 whole orange, sliced
2 quarts sweet white wine	4 oz grapes
2 bottles cream soda	½ pint white rum
Juice of 2 lemons	

Dissolve the sugar in the boiling water and allow to cool. Add all the other ingredients and stir well. Serve to the parish.

WASSAIL

¾ pint water	2 teabags
2 oz demerara sugar	¼ pint cider
1 orange stuck with 10 cloves	¼ pint whisky
1 stick cinnamon	½ pint orange juice
1 tsp lemon juice	

Boil the water and dissolve the sugar in it. Simmer the orange and the stick of cinnamon in it for 5 minutes. Add a teaspoonful of lemon juice. Add the teabags and allow to infuse for a few minutes. Then pour in the cider, whisky and orange juice and simmer for a few minutes more. Float some slices of apple and orange on the top and serve very hot.

Wassailing was the delightful custom of going from house to house to salute your neighbours with a song. In turn you'd be welcomed with a drop of something to warm the cockles – and surely nothing better than this joyous cup.

PINK PARTY CUP

1 bottle rosé wine	3 tbsp orange juice
1 tbsp brandy	¾ pint cream soda

Mix together well in a large jug, and serve with lots of ice. A very good wine cup for a summer party.

ELDERBERRY CORDIAL

2½ lb elderberries	8 oz preserving sugar
Juice of 2 lemons and finely grated rind of 1 lemon	

Carefully remove the elderberries from their stalks using a fork. Put in a saucepan and add the lemon juice.

Heat the berries gently and cook for 1 minute. Crush with a wooden spoon and add the sugar and the finely grated rind of 1 lemon. Simmer until the sugar has dissolved. Strain through muslin or a nylon sieve and bottle. Use like any other cordial, diluting with 3 parts water to 1 part juice.

FR MORGAN'S WEE DRAM

3 eggs	2 tsp vanilla essence
10 fl oz double cream	1 wineglass whisky
1 tbsp coffee essence	

Beat the eggs well and blend with the double cream. Add the rest of the ingredients. Bottle and keep in the refrigerator.

FRUIT CUP

6 oranges	1 pint cold tea
2 lemons	½ pint orange juice
1 tin pineapple chunks, including	4 oz sugar
juice	1 bottle red wine (optional)
1 tin of fruit salad (or use various fresh fruits such as apples, grapes, pears, peaches, cubed)	

Slice the oranges and the lemons into a bowl and add all the other ingredients. Allow to stand for 1 hour. Add ice and serve. If you wish, pour in the bottle of wine just before serving.

LEMONADE

3 pints water	2 lb sugar
3 lemons	2 oz citric acid
1 lime	

Boil the water in a pan and add the grated rinds of the lemons and the lime. Bring the water to the boil and simmer for 1 minute.

Mix the sugar and the citric acid in a large bowl and squeeze on the juice of the lemons and the lime. Pour in the boiling water, stir to dissolve the sugar and allow to cool. Bottle and keep in the refrigerator.

Dilute with 3 parts water to 1 part lemonade.

· INDEX ·